Ben Crow is Professor of Sociology at the University of California Santa Cruz. He is the author of two books, *Markets, Class and Social Change*, and *Sharing the Ganges*, and co-author of four more, including *The Third World Atlas*, and *The Food Question*. His main research is currently on gender and access to water in the Global South. He was a political activist in what was then East Pakistan, now Bangladesh, before he became an academic. He has a BSc in Civil Engineering from Regent Street Polytechnic and a PhD from Edinburgh University.

Suresh K. Lodha is Professor of Computer Science at the University of California Santa Cruz. He has published more than 100 articles in journals and conferences. His research interests include visualization, vision, and social entrepreneurship. He received an Excellence in Teaching Award at UCSC. He received an MSc from IIT, Kanpur (India), an MA from University of California, Berkeley, and a PhD in Computer Science from Rice University.

THE ATLAS OF
GLOBAL
INEQUALITIES

Ben Crow and Suresh K. Lodha

UNIVERSITY OF CALIFORNIA PRESS

Berkeley   Los Angeles   London

University of California Press, one of the most distinguished university presses in the United States, enriches lives around the world by advancing scholarship in the humanities, social sciences, and natural sciences. Its activities are supported by the UC Press Foundation and by philanthropic contributions from individuals and institutions. For more information, visit www.ucpress.edu.

University of California Press
Berkeley and Los Angeles, California
University of California Press, Ltd.
London, England

Library of Congress Control Number: 2010934244
ISBN: 978-0-520-26822-7 (pbk. : alk. paper)

Produced for University of California Press by
Myriad Editions
Brighton, UK
www.MyriadEditions.com

Edited and coordinated by Jannet King, Candida Lacey, and Dawn Sackett
Designed by Isabelle Lewis and Corinne Pearlman
Maps and graphics created by Isabelle Lewis

Printed on paper produced from sustainable sources.
Printed and bound in Hong Kong through Lion Production
under the supervision of Bob Cassels, The Hanway Press, London.

15 14 13 12 11
10 9 8 7 6 5 4 3 2 1

Contents

1 Economic Inequalities   14

2 Power Inequalities   26

3 Social Inequalities   38

4 Inequalities of Access   50

5 Health Inequalities   66

6 Educational Inequalities

Literacy

Poverty, poor quality education, and lack of educational opportunity for girls all influence national literacy levels.

Barriers to Education

Poverty, gender, disability, language, location, and ethnicity constitute major barriers to education.

Early Childhood Care & Education

Children who are denied access to early childhood care and pre-school education suffer a range of health and educational disadvantages.

7 Environmental Inequalities

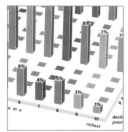

Climate Change

Industrialized countries have historically been the largest carbon emitters, but developing nations and the poor bear the brunt of the resultant climate disasters.

Deforestation

Rapid deforestation is having a negative environmental impact and threatening the livelihoods of a quarter of the world's population.

Air Pollution & Health

Air pollution, both indoors and outdoors, is a significant cause of death and disabling disease.

Water & Health

A tenth of all disease could be alleviated by improvements in household water, sanitation, and water-resource management. The poor are most likely to lack clean water and sanitation services.

8 Towards Equality

9 Data, Definitions & Sources

Acknowledgments

The following people provided background research on specific topics:

Sachi Allen	*Income, Child Labor, Poverty, Household Water*
Courtney Codd	*Gender*
Meghan Lefkowitz	*Child Labor*
Patricia Fung	*Consumption, Life Expectancy*
Meena Garg	*Age*
Sandeep Gill	*International Trade, Access to Healthcare*
Jenna Harvey	*Hunger, Literacy, Barriers to Education*
Lucas Healy	*Digital Divide*
James Issel	*Energy, Household Fuel, Mobility*
Taralyn Kawata	*Labor Migration, Freedom & Democracy, Race & Ethnicity*
Madhu Lodha	*Early Childhood Care & Education, Age*
Jasmine Lopez	*Government Action, Class, Infectious Diseases*
Cory Mann	*Air Pollution & Health, Water & Health*
Patrick O'Connell	*Climate Change, Deforestation*
Sarah Orr	*Budget Priorities*
Issac Rigler	*Incarceration & Execution*
Erin Stephens	*HDI, Wealth, Work & Unemployment*
Nichole Zlatunich	*Maternal Mortality, Child Mortality*

In addition, several people deserve special mention: Nichole Zlatunich for her ideas, enthusiasm and authorship in the early months of this and preceding projects; the team at Myriad Editions, including Jannet King for so ably steering the project through a transatlantic flow of editorial suggestions and comments, assisted by Dawn Sackett, Isabelle Lewis for transforming the data into elegant graphics, and Candida Lacey and Corinne Pearlman for their helpful co-operation; Bob Sutcliffe for providing many sources, ideas and frequent advice; Brian Fulfrost for his coordination and work on the online UC Atlas of Global Inequality; participants in the Mapping Global Inequalities conference at UCSC in 2007; Martha Ramirez and others at the UCSC Library for their rapid responses; students in Sociology 171 Global Inequalities in Fall 2009 for their work on early drafts.

Many others provided advice and assistance, including: Amit Basol, Tom Bassett, Henry Bernstein, Laura Cerruti, Carol Colfer, James Davies, Hannah Engholm, James K. Galbraith, Paul Hewett, Corrinne Hughes, Marlene Kim, Anirudh Krishna, Edith Kuiper, Cynthia Lloyd, Allister McGregor, Maureen Mackintosh, Branko Milanovic, Lisa Nishioka. Ravi Rajan, Craig Reinarman, Anthony Shorrocks, William Sunderlin, Brent Swallow, Göran Therborn, M. Ufuk Tutan, Ed Wolff.

Ben Crow would like to thank and express his appreciation for his children Sam Crow and Eleanor Crow.

Suresh Lodha would like to express his gratitude towards his spouse Madhu Lodha, without whose unwavering support this work would never have come to fruition.

Introduction

What is inequality?

The goal of equality expresses the idea that each person should have comparable freedoms across a range of dimensions. Inequalities are, then, constraints that hinder accomplishment of those freedoms. There is debate about which dimensions of freedom should be prioritized. At the same time, however, there is substantial global common ground that deprivations below a range of achievements constitute unacceptable inequality. This common ground is formulated, most obviously, in the Millennium Development Goals, but also in the Universal Declaration of Human Rights (1948), and in the constitutions of many nations.

Another way of answering the question "What is inequality?" comes from sociologist Göran Therborn (2006: 4): inequalities are differences we consider unjust. Humans are diverse, and social conditions across the planet vary, but are raised to the level of injustice – an inequality – when they violate a moral norm and when, as Therborn puts it, the inequality is capable of being changed (2009: 20). When 2 percent of adults possess more than half of all global wealth, when one child in seven dies before the age of five in Sub-Saharan Africa, when one in five girl children is allowed to die young, or is selectively aborted, as happens in China, many consider that unjust.

Theories of ethics and justice, from the Left and the Right of the political spectrum, demand equality in one dimension or another in order to speak plausibly to all (Sen 1992). Even theories that argue against equality are concerned with some dimension of inequality.

> Not only do income-egalitarians ... demand equal incomes, and welfare-egalitarians ask for equal welfare levels, but also ... pure libertarians demand equality with respect to an entire class of rights and liberties. They are all "egalitarians" in some essential way ... (Sen 1992: ix)

So, economist and philosopher Amartya Sen argues that ethical and political theories debate not egalitarianism versus freedom, but what dimension of equality should be sought.

This atlas broadens the debate from a narrow definition of inequality that focuses on inequality of income because we suspect that specific dimensions of inequality have causes and possible mitigations related to that dimension. Nonetheless, there are some general processes behind a range of inequalities.

What causes inequality?

While inequalities are often palpable daily experiences for the injured individual, the causes may be multiple and complex. Therborn (2006, 2009) has, nonetheless, suggested a useful fourfold summary of key causes of inequality (which we simplify):

> *Exploitation* – the extraction of value by a superior group from an inferior group, for example, employers using low-paid labor;
> *Exclusion* – discrimination by one group excluding another, for example, racism;
> *Distantiation* – economic mechanisms, such as the bonus

culture, that result in a widening distance between low-ranking employees and executives, countries that are not industrializing and those that are;

Hierarchy – advantages within formal organizations, such as rank within an administration, corporation, or army.

These causes of inequality arise both from an individual's initial endowments, of skill and fortune, and from their location in systems of opportunities structured by nation, class, gender, and race. They operate through institutions, such as a corporation or a family, through practices of interaction, including labor hiring, housing allocation, and the borrowing and lending of money, and through the language we use to explain, think about and enact our daily lives. They are, in other words, dispersed throughout all elements of human existence, and they may influence action at all levels, from face-to-face contact to national and international dealings.

One pattern evident from the map of the Human Development Index, and throughout the pages of this atlas, is the difference between those who live in the industrialized "North" of the globe, and those who live in the non-industrialized "South". With few exceptions, birth in a non-industrialized (developing) nation predisposes two-thirds of the world's population to disadvantage in almost all dimensions of inequality. This happens because the growth of industrial productivity transforms many aspects of society, and the life possibilities of most, if not all, in that nation.

We can identify this process as the *distantiation* of the North from the South, involving also elements of *exploitation* and *exclusion* during and since colonial rule. The evidence from historical studies of income and economic production (see pages 16–17) suggests that increasing productivity as the North industrialized was the main force driving this distantiation. There is an irony or paradox that North–South distantiation continues in the 21st century, even as travel and communication times are reduced by technological innovation.

Analytical approach

The analytical approach that informs this atlas is that of Amartya Sen. In his work on inequality, famine and poverty (1981, 1992, 1999), Sen distinguished some useful analytical categories:

Entitlements and capabilities – social and individual relations giving command over a desired functioning, for example, employment of laborers, which entitles them to a wage with which to buy food;

Functionings – desired individual outcomes such as a long life or being nourished;

Freedoms – a broad set, including political freedoms, economic facilities, social opportunities, transparency guarantees, and protective security.

Functionings and freedoms are things that people want to do and to be. In other words, Sen describes inequalities in relation to desirable achievements, the lives that people value. Then, his analysis identifies the specific entitlements and capabilities that enable a particular

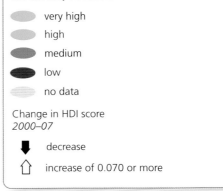

▲ **HUMAN DEVELOPMENT INDEX**
2007

The Human Development Index combines three elements: longevity measured by life expectancy at birth, income measured by GDP per capita, and knowledge measured by adult literacy rate, school, and university enrollment.

very high

high

medium

low

no data

Change in HDI score
2000–07

⬇ decrease

⇧ increase of 0.070 or more

outcome. Most strikingly, this approach has been applied to reconceptualize social advance or development:

> Expansion of freedom is viewed, in this approach, both as the primary end and as the principal means of development. Development consists of the removal of various types of unfreedoms that leave people with little choice and little opportunity of exercising their reasoned agency. (Sen 1999; xii)

These ideas have helped make a significant opening for human advancement, and helped foster an analysis that rescued the tragedy of famine from scholarly and governmental indifference. The ideas of entitlements and capabilities helped disaggregate social relationships, providing new language for interdisciplinary understanding of, and action on, this most desperate of human crises. Recognition of the importance of achieved functionings, notably life expectancy, provided new ways of thinking about progress. This spurred wide global debate, notably among government agencies, and led to new measures of social progress. The idea of plural freedoms, criticism notwithstanding (Agarwal, Humphries and Robeyns 2005: 8-9), has helped revitalize the study of social change, and facilitated analysis and action to recognize and mitigate multidimensional inequality.

There is, as Therborn notes, a need to make this analytical approach more accessible and useful for empirical research. Ideas of entitlement, capability, functionings and freedoms are not easily understood or measured. They provide a way of disaggregating human achievements, the lives we want, and the complex social and physical processes that produce them.

In this atlas, the analytical approach helps to illuminate the multiple dimensions of inequality, and an exploration of current understanding of the social dynamics of each. To make sense of the many dimensions of inequality, the atlas is structured around a set of categories based on terms in common usage.

Human Development Index

In 1990, the UN Development Program, one of the UN's less influential agencies, engaged one of the most powerful (the World Bank) in a discussion about how to represent human achievement. At stake was whether progress should be measured by the proliferation of goods, or by the length and quality of people's lives. The UNDP, drawing partly on ideas from Amartya Sen, proposed measuring human achievement with the Human Development Index, an aggregate measure combining life expectancy, literacy and an improved indicator of productivity (GDP per capita at Purchasing Power Parity – see page 118 for definition). No single indicator is adequate to represent the multiple dimensions of global inequality, but the HDI has opened up discussion of social priorities. The HDI reveals the importance of action, usually governmental or collective, through programs that redistribute, include, and protect the interests of the disadvantaged.

The diagram (right) demonstrates that there is not necessarily a direct correlation between national income and human development. Saudi Arabia, for example, is famously rich from oil royalties, but achieves less for its citizens in terms of life expectancy and literacy than does Cuba, with one-third the GDP per capita. Countries with similar national incomes per capita, such as Armenia, Egypt, and Angola, have HDI scores that are very different. This reinforces the point that government action for the disadvantaged matters.

On the whole, however, industrialized areas of North America and Europe tend to have a high HDI, while non-industrialized, developing, areas of Africa and South America have lower HDI, as is evident from the map on pages 10–11. Social action in countries with low levels of income can raise their HDI scores to match the scores of countries with higher income primarily by reducing inequality and increasing the efficacy of spending on health and education.

Although most countries' HDI score has been increasing, inequalities between rural and urban areas persist, especially in those countries, such as China, where the national economy is booming. The rural population in every province of China experiences worse living conditions, on average, than those registered as urban (which

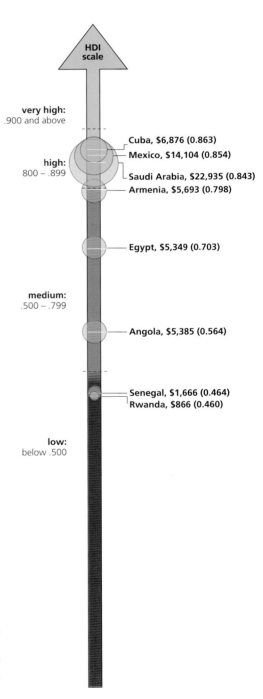

▼ COMPARISON OF INCOME AND HUMAN DEVELOPMENT
GDP per capita PPP$
HDI score for selected countries

size of GDP per capita PPP$ 2007 (HDI score)

HDI scale

very high: .900 and above

Cuba, $6,876 (0.863)
Mexico, $14,104 (0.854)

high: .800 – .899

Saudi Arabia, $22,935 (0.843)
Armenia, $5,693 (0.798)

Egypt, $5,349 (0.703)

medium: .500 – .799

Angola, $5,385 (0.564)

Senegal, $1,666 (0.464)
Rwanda, $866 (0.460)

low: below .500

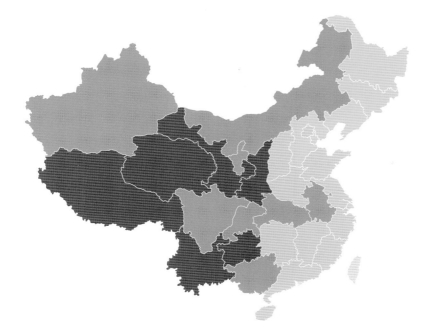

◄ RURAL–URBAN DIVIDE IN CHINA
Difference in rural and urban HDI score
within provinces of China *2003*

- 150 – 208 *least equal*
- 125 – 149
- 100 – 124
- 80 – 99 *most equal*
- no data

There is a large disparity in access to
healthcare and education between
China's rural and urban population,
most evident in the provinces of the
more rural western region. In the
rapidly urbanizing eastern provinces,
the disparity is less marked.

does not include rural migrants working in towns and cities).
The greatest discrepancy between rural and urban is found in the
predominantly rural provinces.

Critics of the HDI question the reliance on only three dimensions
of human development to indicate human capabilities and well-
being. They also assert that failure to include ecological and gender
considerations renders HDI an inadequate measure of human
development. It is clear, nonetheless, that the discussion begun in
1990 by publication of the first *Human Development Report*, has
created space for a broader conception of human goals than was
prevalent at that time.

Problems with the national view

The genre of the global statistical atlas, of which this is an example,
rests on the growth of international agencies, with first the League
of Nations and then the United Nations, and their need to publish
compilations of national statistics that illustrate the scale of the issues
they address.

There are risks in the use of these statistics. Constant repetition
of global maps can reinforce the simple idea that nations are the
appropriate and exclusive unit for analyzing inequalities and social
change. We have sought to mitigate this risk through the use of
graphs, maps, and charts that illustrate differences along lines of
gender, class or ethnicity, and through the occasional use of spatial
distributions within one country.

We leave the reader to remember the differences within her or his
own nation, to be unsatisfied by national averages, and to question
ideas that nations rather than people organize social change.

Ben Crow
Suresh Lodha
Santa Cruz, August 2010

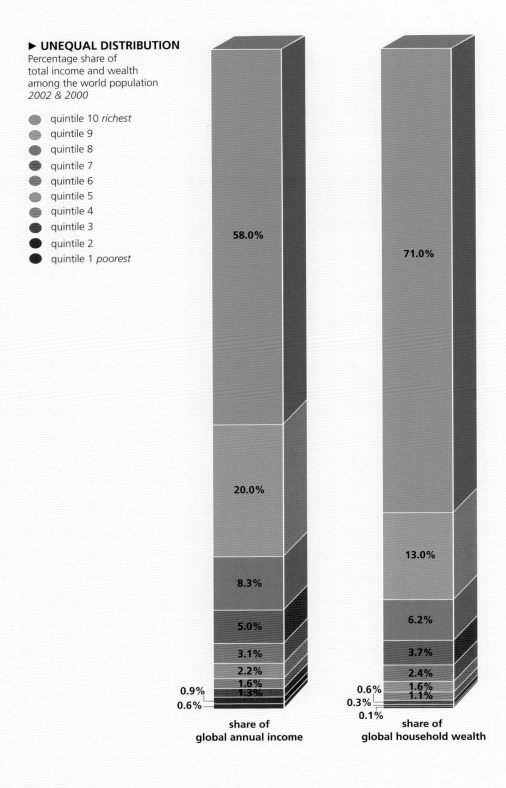

▶ **UNEQUAL DISTRIBUTION**
Percentage share of
total income and wealth
among the world population
2002 & 2000

- quintile 10 *richest*
- quintile 9
- quintile 8
- quintile 7
- quintile 6
- quintile 5
- quintile 4
- quintile 3
- quintile 2
- quintile 1 *poorest*

58.0%

20.0%

8.3%

5.0%

3.1%

2.2%

1.6%

0.9%

1.3%

0.6%

**share of
global annual income**

71.0%

13.0%

6.2%

3.7%

2.4%

1.6%

0.6%

1.1%

0.3%

0.1%

**share of
global household wealth**

14

Economic Inequalities   1

▶ Economic differences are the most common focus of study and comment, partly because they are most easily measured. They are given prominence at the beginning of this atlas, however, because they are a major underlying driver of many of the social inequalities covered in the rest of the book.

The wealthiest tenth of the global population receives 58 percent of annual incomes, and owns 71 percent of household wealth – assets, property and capital. And while the average income of the richest decile is 94 times that of the poorest, the ratio between the average household wealth of the richest and poorest deciles is an almost unimaginable 175,750:1.

Redressing the negative effects of income and wealth inequality is complicated, not least because the social processes involved in raising productivity and living standards also create inequalities. The global system of capitalism has been successful in harnessing technical and social innovation to generate increased productivity. This has enabled higher living standards, notably in the industrial countries but much less so in the developing world. This uneven pattern of industrialization is the main reason why income inequality between countries rose from about 3:1 in 1800 to 72:1 in 1992.

Capitalism also generates inequalities within countries, giving some great wealth, others meager wages, and still others unemployment. Although some parts of Europe have less income inequality than the USA or Brazil, the extent to which capitalism is compatible with economic equality is debatable. Capitalism operates through the accumulation of wealth in the hands of a few – a process that is speeded by low wages and unemployment. Currently, 2 percent of the world's population owns half the world's wealth. Huge armies of the poor face insecurity and low returns in the informal sector in Asia, Africa and Latin America.

The processes of accumulation and exploitation interact with many other causes of inequality, including exclusions such as racism, to create diverse patterns of wealth, consumption, work, and unemployment. In turn, these inequalities constrain many individual freedoms and capabilities. The rich, to give an obvious example, have command over magnificent homes, art, culture, beauty, and much else besides, while most of the poor cannot keep their food cold.

Economic inequality can be reduced through labor migration, although barriers to mobility are especially high for poor people, and people with low skills, despite the demand for their labor in many rich countries. Sadly, forces of exclusion, such as racism and nationalism, stand in the way of the equalizing potential of migration. All rich countries have erected barriers against people crossing borders to seek work.

Income

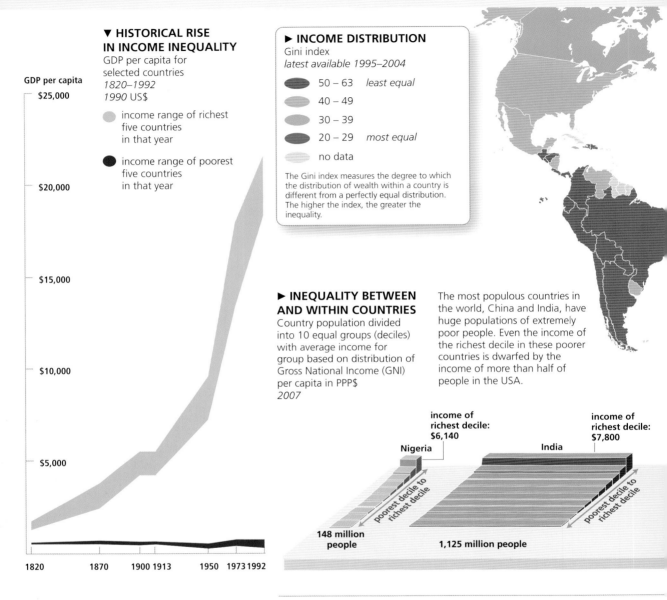

▼ HISTORICAL RISE IN INCOME INEQUALITY

GDP per capita for selected countries
1820–1992
1990 US$

- income range of richest five countries in that year
- income range of poorest five countries in that year

GDP per capita

- $25,000
- $20,000
- $15,000
- $10,000
- $5,000

1820   1870   1900 1913   1950   1973 1992

► INCOME DISTRIBUTION

Gini index
latest available 1995–2004

- 50 – 63   *least equal*
- 40 – 49
- 30 – 39
- 20 – 29   *most equal*
- no data

The Gini index measures the degree to which the distribution of wealth within a country is different from a perfectly equal distribution. The higher the index, the greater the inequality.

► INEQUALITY BETWEEN AND WITHIN COUNTRIES

Country population divided into 10 equal groups (deciles) with average income for group based on distribution of Gross National Income (GNI) per capita in PPP$
2007

The most populous countries in the world, China and India, have huge populations of extremely poor people. Even the income of the richest decile in these poorer countries is dwarfed by the income of more than half of people in the USA.

Nigeria
income of richest decile: $6,140
148 million people
poorest decile to richest decile

India
income of richest decile: $7,800
1,125 million people
poorest decile to richest decile

In 1820 the ratio between incomes in richest and poorest countries was roughly
3:1
By 1992 it was
72:1

► Most debates about global inequality focus on income inequality. National incomes can be measured using Gross Domestic Product – the total of goods and services produced in that economy – or Gross National Income (GNI), which includes income earned outside the country. These are measures of output or the value of production, not wages, but when divided by the number of people in the country they roughly equate to the average individual's ability to buy goods, to their standard of living. Combining this with data on income distribution within a country creates a powerful picture of economic inequalities.

Income inequality between countries grew in the last 200 years as some countries industrialized. Industry produces cheaper goods and pays better wages than farming. Until the beginning of the 19th century, income (GDP

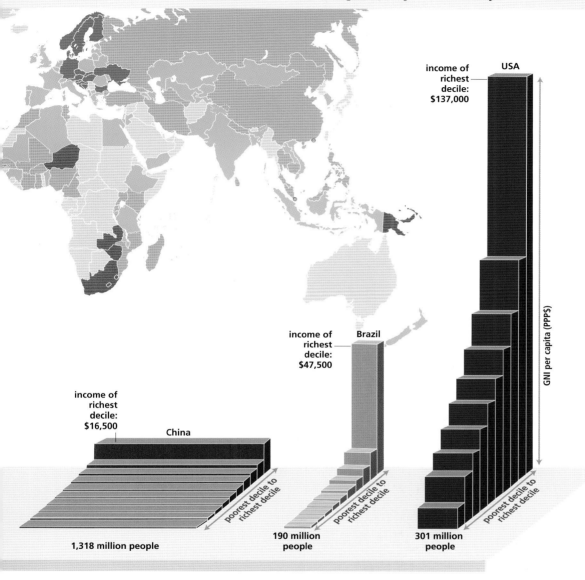

income of richest decile: $137,000 — USA

income of richest decile: $47,500 — Brazil

income of richest decile: $16,500 — China

GNI per capita (PPP$)

poorest decile to richest decile

1,318 million people

190 million people

301 million people

per capita) differences between countries were relatively small, but the industrializing countries pulled ahead of societies that depended primarily on agriculture, and a large income gap opened up.

Income inequality within a country can be measured by the Gini coefficient. South America is notable for its high level of inequality, while the countries of Scandinavia and Eastern Europe, albeit with very different economic histories, have the most equal income distribution.

The industrialization of China and India is beginning to raise average incomes in those countries, although inequalities within both countries are growing. Many economies in Africa and Asia are building industrial capabilities only slowly, however, and the gap between average incomes in those countries and the industrialized west continues to rise.

In the USA the average income of the richest tenth of the population is
17 times
that of the poorest tenth

Household Wealth

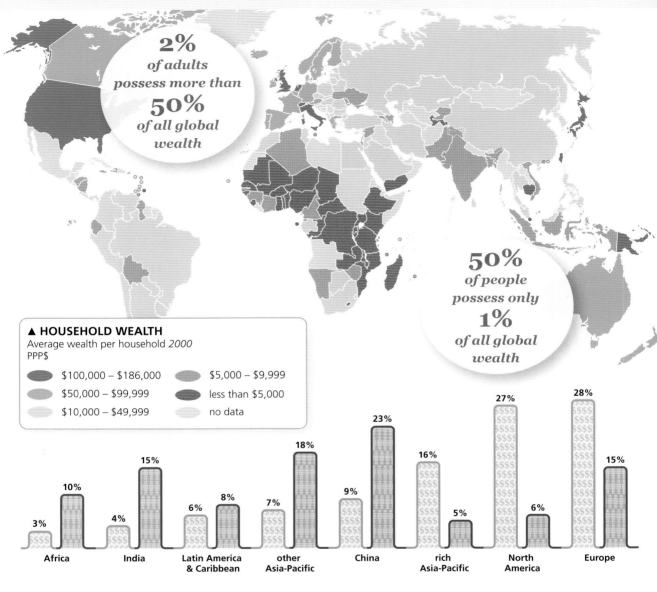

2% *of adults possess more than* **50%** *of all global wealth*

50% *of people possess only* **1%** *of all global wealth*

▲ HOUSEHOLD WEALTH
Average wealth per household *2000*
PPP$

- $100,000 – $186,000
- $50,000 – $99,999
- $10,000 – $49,999
- $5,000 – $9,999
- less than $5,000
- no data

Region	Share
Africa	3% / 10%
India	4% / 15%
Latin America & Caribbean	6% / 8%
other Asia-Pacific	7% / 18%
China	9% / 23%
rich Asia-Pacific	16% / 5%
North America	27% / 6%
Europe	28% / 15%

▲ SHARE OF GLOBAL POPULATION AND WEALTH
2000
PPP exchange rates

- share of global wealth
- share of adult population

► Household wealth – the total value of physical and financial assets, including dwellings, livestock and land, less any debt – is highly concentrated. In 2000, around 10 percent of the world's population possessed over 85 percent of world wealth.

Research on economic inequality predominantly focuses on disparities of income or consumption, yet the distribution of household wealth is even more unequal than that of income. Wealth is accumulated over time, so income differences tend to be amplified.

An assessment of household wealth provides different insights from those gained from measurements of income. Wealth enables poor households, for example, to survive unexpected events such as a natural disaster or prolonged illness, which might adversely affect their ability to

Household wealth is unevenly distributed across the world. A huge proportion is concentrated in the hands of a very few.

▼ DISTRIBUTION OF GLOBAL WEALTH

World adult population grouped according to wealth, colored by region

2000

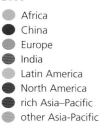

- Africa
- China
- Europe
- India
- Latin America
- North America
- rich Asia–Pacific
- other Asia-Pacific

The bar chart below displays the distribution of wealth across the world. Each group of bars represents a tenth (a decile) of the world's adult population (370 million), from the poorest decile on the left, to the wealthiest decile on the right. The colors indicate in which regions of the world people in different wealth deciles live.

Latin America has a fairly equal number of adults in each wealth decile, indicating that wealth is quite evenly distributed. The bars for Africa vary more in height, indicating unequally distributed wealth, with the majority of people in the poorest deciles. The bars for North America also range widely in height, but the majority of people are in the richest deciles.

The single bar on the right, represents the wealthiest 370 million adults in the world, and is divided up to indicate which countries they inhabit.

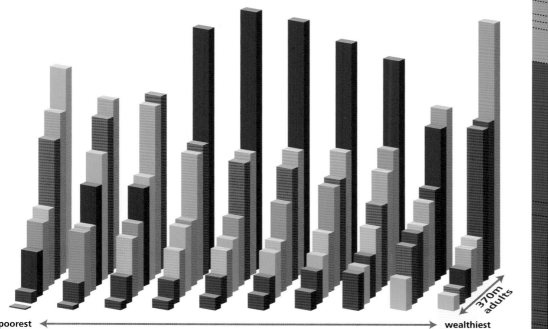

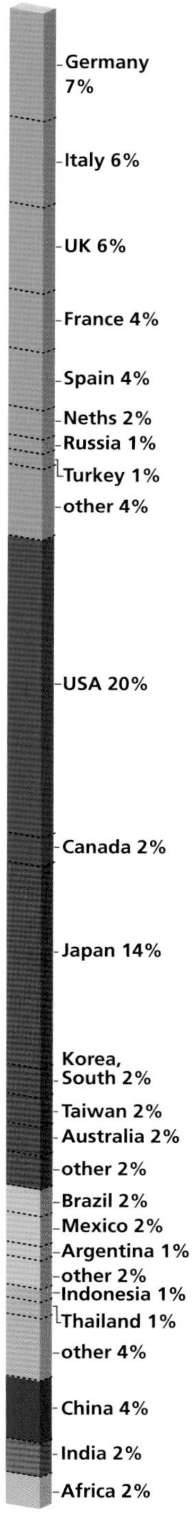

370m adults
poorest
wealthiest

Germany 7%
Italy 6%
UK 6%
France 4%
Spain 4%
Neths 2%
Russia 1%
Turkey 1%
other 4%
USA 20%
Canada 2%
Japan 14%
Korea, South 2%
Taiwan 2%
Australia 2%
other 2%
Brazil 2%
Mexico 2%
Argentina 1%
other 2%
Indonesia 1%
Thailand 1%
other 4%
China 4%
India 2%
Africa 2%

Wealthiest tenth of the world's adults

provide for family members. While some assets, like livestock, may be vulnerable in a natural disaster, others, like land, may enable households to generate money for their survival.

Most households in the world own very little. A household with more than $2,100 is in the top half of the global distribution. China dominates the fourth to eighth deciles in the global wealth distribution because the ownership of land, housing and other goods is more equal, partly as a result of socialist land reforms, than in other areas such as South Asia.

Improvements in the quality and collection of wealth-related data is badly needed for further studies, especially in those countries in Africa, Asia, and South America where household balance sheets were not available for the 2000 survey.

Consumption

▼ UNEQUAL CONSUMPTION

Share of world expenditure
on consumable goods
by the world's richest fifth
and poorest fifth
2005

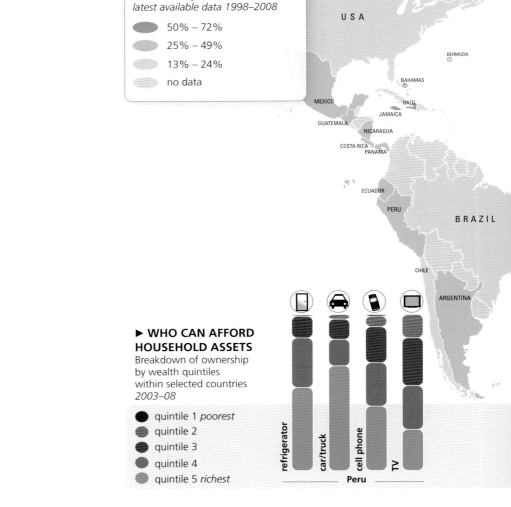

77%

1.5%

richest
fifth

poorest
fifth

► EXPENDITURE ON FOOD

As a percentage of
household expenditure on
consumable goods
latest available data 1998–2008

- 50% – 72%
- 25% – 49%
- 13% – 24%
- no data

CANADA

USA

BERMUDA

BAHAMAS

MEXICO

HAITI

JAMAICA

GUATEMALA

NICARAGUA

COSTA RICA

PANAMA

ECUADOR

PERU

BRAZIL

CHILE

ARGENTINA

► WHO CAN AFFORD HOUSEHOLD ASSETS

Breakdown of ownership
by wealth quintiles
within selected countries
2003–08

- ● quintile 1 *poorest*
- ● quintile 2
- ● quintile 3
- ● quintile 4
- ● quintile 5 *richest*

refrigerator

car/truck

cell phone

TV

Peru

► Inequalities in global spending are stark. The richest fifth of the world's population are responsible for 77 percent of all spending by households on goods and services, and the poorest fifth a miniscule 1.5 percent – a distribution that has barely changed since the mid-1990s.

For a household to have an adequate standard of living, it needs to spend money on food, clothing, housing, medical care, and education. However, many poor households are forced to spend a large share – an average of over 50 percent in many low-income countries – of their income on food alone. By contrast, in high-income, industrialized countries, expenditure on food might represent only 10 percent of household income, although the actual amount spent may be more than 10 times greater than the amount spent by those in poorer countries.

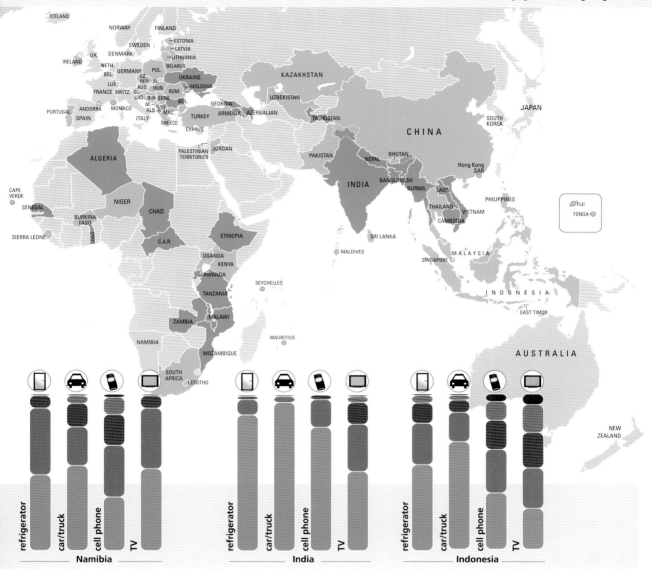

People face deprivation even in industrialized countries, where more than 100 million people are reported homeless. In the USA, where more food is consumed per person than anywhere else in the world, nearly 7 million households reported going hungry at some point during 2008.

In non-industrialized countries, about a fifth of all people are undernourished, and a quarter do not have adequate housing. Ownership of household assets such as refrigerators, televisions, cell phones and cars is concentrated in the wealthiest groups.

Raising the consumption levels of more than a billion poor people is as important as moving towards sustainable consumption patterns that reduce environmental damage and promote product safety and the rights of consumers.

*The richest fifth
own*
87%
*of the world's
motor vehicles;
the poorest fifth own
less than 1%*

Work & Unemployment

▼ GENDER DIFFERENCES IN UNEMPLOYMENT

▼ GENDER DIFFERENCES IN UNEMPLOYMENT

Female unemployment as percentage of male unemployment
1996–2005

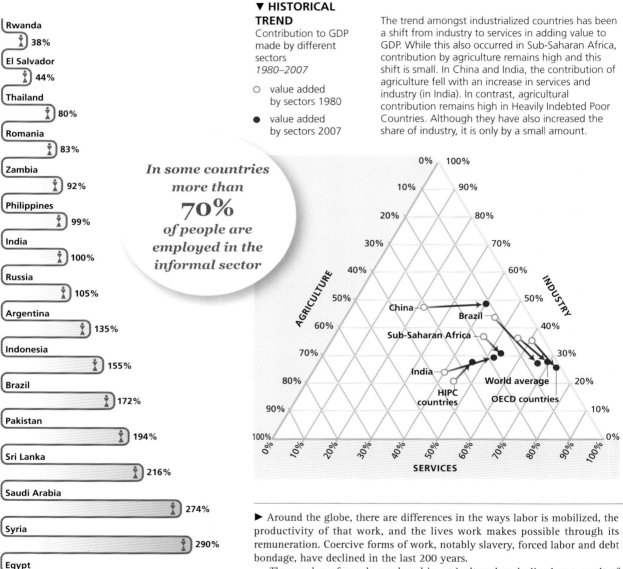

Rwanda
👤 38%

El Salvador
👤 44%

Thailand
👤 80%

Romania
👤 83%

Zambia
👤 92%

Philippines
👤 99%

India
👤 100%

Russia
👤 105%

Argentina
👤 135%

Indonesia
👤 155%

Brazil
👤 172%

Pakistan
👤 194%

Sri Lanka
👤 216%

Saudi Arabia
👤 274%

Syria
👤 290%

Egypt
👤 311%

Ethiopia
👤 312%

Belarus
👤 325%

In some countries more than **70%** *of people are employed in the informal sector*

▼ HISTORICAL TREND
Contribution to GDP made by different sectors
1980–2007

○ value added by sectors 1980

● value added by sectors 2007

The trend amongst industrialized countries has been a shift from industry to services in adding value to GDP. While this also occurred in Sub-Saharan Africa, contribution by agriculture remains high and this shift is small. In China and India, the contribution of agriculture fell with an increase in services and industry (in India). In contrast, agricultural contribution remains high in Heavily Indebted Poor Countries. Although they have also increased the share of industry, it is only by a small amount.

AGRICULTURE — INDUSTRY — SERVICES

China
Brazil
Sub-Saharan Africa
India
HIPC countries
World average
OECD countries

▶ Around the globe, there are differences in the ways labor is mobilized, the productivity of that work, and the lives work makes possible through its remuneration. Coercive forms of work, notably slavery, forced labor and debt bondage, have declined in the last 200 years.

The number of people employed in agriculture has declined as a result of mechanization and the increasing number of jobs in manufacturing, mining, power generation, and construction. More recently, the more "advanced" economies have moved away from the manufacture of goods, towards the provision of services such as marketing, finance, and legal expertise. A comparison of the proportion of people employed in agriculture, industry and services, and the contribution those sectors make to a country's GDP, reveals the contribution made by workers in each sector to the economy.

▼ COMPARATIVE PRODUCTIVITY

Percentage employed in and value added to GDP by agriculture, industry, and service sectors *2007*

□ employment

● value added to GDP

— Africa
— Asia
— Europe
— Latin America
— Middle East
— OECD countries

Developing countries tend to have a higher proportion of their population employed in agriculture than in the other two sectors. But agriculture does not add as much to the economy as industry and services do. Long lines (from employment to value added) suggest that people employed in one sector, usually agriculture, contribute less to the economy than those in other sectors.

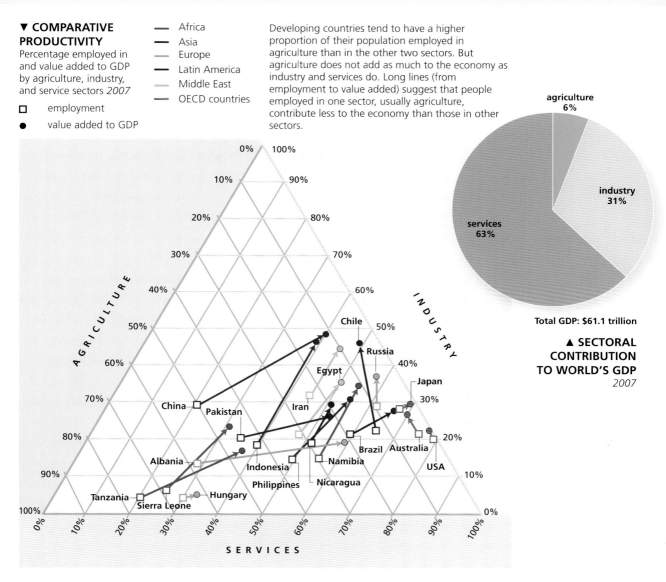

Total GDP: $61.1 trillion

▲ SECTORAL CONTRIBUTION TO WORLD'S GDP
2007

Most people in industrialized economies work in formal, contracted, regulated employment, but in most developing countries the majority work informally, in unregulated work, producing and selling goods on a small scale. The nature of this work makes reliable data hard to find.

Unemployment is a major source of inequality and deprivation, particularly throughout most of the non-industrial world, where there is little support for the unemployed. Unemployment levels have risen dramatically since the onset of the recession in 2007, but global data on this change is not yet available.

Work provides more than remuneration. It may, for example, bestow status. Gender differences in the level of unemployment often reflect power inequalities – most strikingly in the Middle East.

In some countries
60% *are employed in agriculture but contribute only* **20%** *of GDP*

Labor Migration

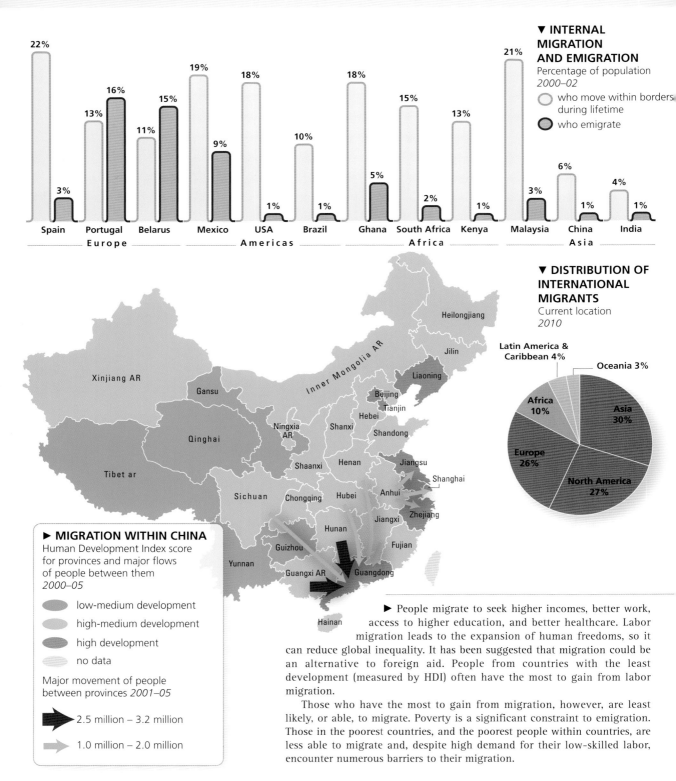

▼ INTERNAL MIGRATION AND EMIGRATION
Percentage of population
2000–02

◯ who move within borders during lifetime

⬤ who emigrate

Europe
- Spain 22% / 3%
- Portugal 13% / 16%
- Belarus 11% / 15%

Americas
- Mexico 19% / 9%
- USA 18% / 1%
- Brazil 10% / 1%

Africa
- Ghana 18% / 5%
- South Africa 15% / 2%
- Kenya 13% / 1%

Asia
- Malaysia 21% / 3%
- China 6% / 1%
- India 4% / 1%

▼ DISTRIBUTION OF INTERNATIONAL MIGRANTS
Current location
2010

- Latin America & Caribbean 4%
- Oceania 3%
- Asia 30%
- Africa 10%
- Europe 26%
- North America 27%

▶ MIGRATION WITHIN CHINA
Human Development Index score for provinces and major flows of people between them
2000–05

- low-medium development
- high-medium development
- high development
- no data

Major movement of people between provinces 2001–05

- 2.5 million – 3.2 million
- 1.0 million – 2.0 million

▶ People migrate to seek higher incomes, better work, access to higher education, and better healthcare. Labor migration leads to the expansion of human freedoms, so it can reduce global inequality. It has been suggested that migration could be an alternative to foreign aid. People from countries with the least development (measured by HDI) often have the most to gain from labor migration.

Those who have the most to gain from migration, however, are least likely, or able, to migrate. Poverty is a significant constraint to emigration. Those in the poorest countries, and the poorest people within countries, are less able to migrate and, despite high demand for their low-skilled labor, encounter numerous barriers to their migration.

Each year millions of people move within their own country and between countries in search of better-paid or more secure work. Labor migration can help address global inequalities.

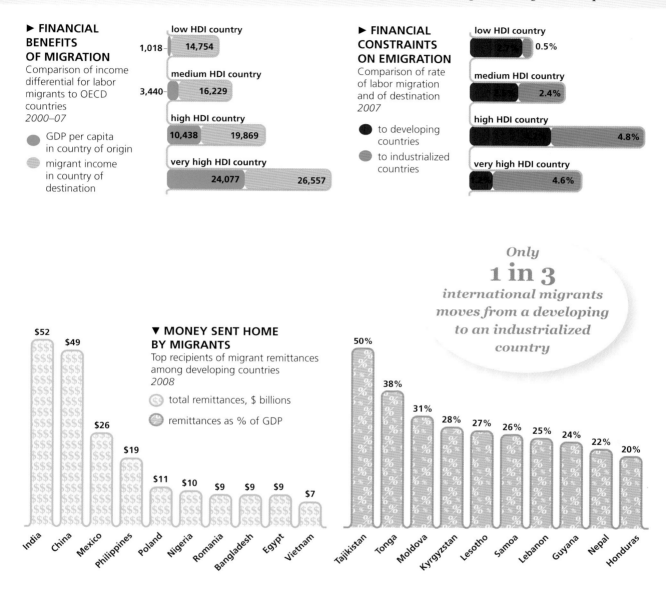

▶ **FINANCIAL BENEFITS OF MIGRATION**

Comparison of income differential for labor migrants to OECD countries
2000–07

- ● GDP per capita in country of origin
- ● migrant income in country of destination

low HDI country
1,018 — 14,754

medium HDI country
3,440 — 16,229

high HDI country
10,438 — 19,869

very high HDI country
24,077 — 26,557

▶ **FINANCIAL CONSTRAINTS ON EMIGRATION**

Comparison of rate of labor migration and of destination
2007

- ● to developing countries
- ● to industrialized countries

low HDI country
2.7% — 0.5%

medium HDI country
— 2.4%

high HDI country
— 4.8%

very high HDI country
— 4.6%

▼ **MONEY SENT HOME BY MIGRANTS**

Top recipients of migrant remittances among developing countries
2008

- ● total remittances, $ billions
- ● remittances as % of GDP

$52 India
$49 China
$26 Mexico
$19 Philippines
$11 Poland
$10 Nigeria
$9 Romania
$9 Bangladesh
$9 Egypt
$7 Vietnam

50% Tajikistan
38% Tonga
31% Moldova
28% Kyrgyzstan
27% Lesotho
26% Samoa
25% Lebanon
24% Guyana
22% Nepal
20% Honduras

Only
1 in 3
international migrants moves from a developing to an industrialized country

Those who do migrate achieve higher incomes than those who stay home. They are able to send money home as remittances, which directly increases opportunities and freedoms for their families. Globally, the money that migrants send home is more than twice as large as foreign aid, and for many countries remittances are the largest source of foreign exchange.

Not everyone who migrates does so for economic purposes. Conflict-induced migration and forced migration also contribute to the overall flows of labor migration. There were some 42 million forcibly displaced people worldwide at the end of 2008.

International migrants:
214 million
Internal migrants:
740 million

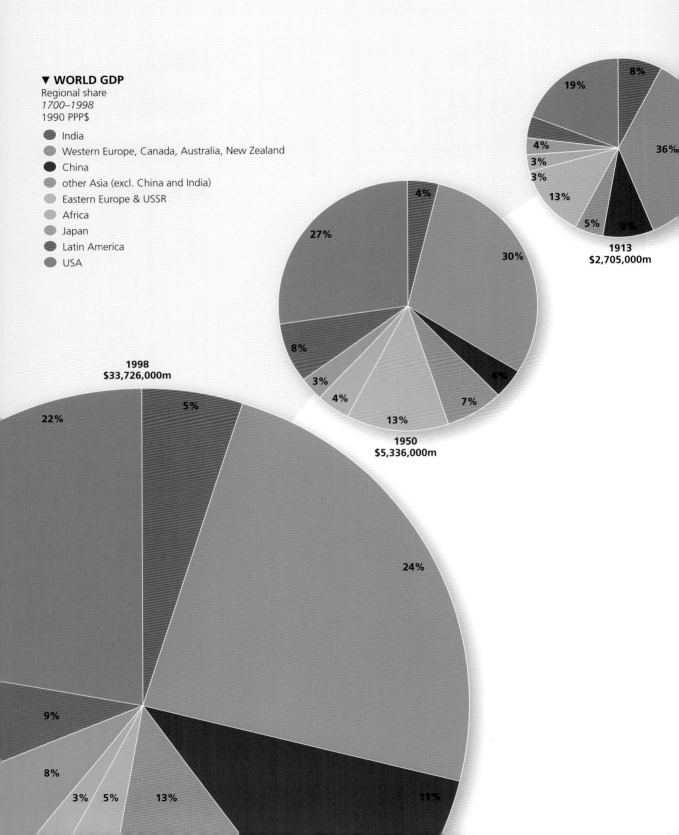

▼ **WORLD GDP**
Regional share
1700–1998
1990 PPP$

- India
- Western Europe, Canada, Australia, New Zealand
- China
- other Asia (excl. China and India)
- Eastern Europe & USSR
- Africa
- Japan
- Latin America
- USA

1913
$2,705,000m

8%
19%
4%
3%
3%
13%
5%
9%
36%

1950
$5,336,000m

4%
27%
30%
8%
3%
4%
13%
7%
4%

1998
$33,726,000m

22%
5%
24%
9%
8%
3% 5% 13% 11%

Power Inequalities 2

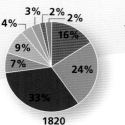

1820
$694,000m

1700
$371,000m

▶ The division of the world into bounded societies under the authority of national governments, which emerged over the last two centuries, has been challenged in the last few decades by the growing interconnectedness of people and their activities. This process of global integration has diverse implications, from the apparent diminution of the power of national governments, through the rise of new global financial and environmental challenges, to questions about the adequacy of global representation, and the rising importance of global economic discourse and ideology.

Nonetheless, national governments remain the dominant actors, and those that have industrialized are the most influential, with global power roughly corresponding to overall economic output. Fueled by the industrial revolution, the share of the world GDP contributed by the West has grown over the last two centuries, but since the beginning of the 21st century the hierarchy of power has begun to change with the rapid industrialization of the two massive economies of China and India. Countries that have been unable to industrialize have much less influence. Those with only a small number of exportable goods face an uphill struggle for foreign exchange and industrialization.

The government of the largest economy, the USA, frequently acts as if it were the government of the world. On other occasions, self-appointed groups of industrialized countries, the G5, G8, and G20, make global decisions on certain topics, while avoiding discussion of others. Thus, these governments exercise ideological power by influencing the framework of desires and goals. They control the public agenda, and dominate international agreements on issues such as trade tariffs, intellectual property laws, agricultural subsidies, international aid, and military assistance.

Military spending dwarfs spending on health and education in many countries. In OECD countries, it also overshadowed development assistance by a factor of around 10:1 in 2005. Greater possibilities for increased freedom and capabilities can emerge at local, national, and global levels if expenditure is directed to the improvement of equality of daily living conditions and security.

The most intimate forms of power, in the home, over language and at work, are also influenced by government action and global ideas. These forms of power are difficult to map, although this section does explore how the power of citizens influences government, through the rise of democratic forms of government, and how the modern state exercises social control via imprisonment and execution.

International Trade

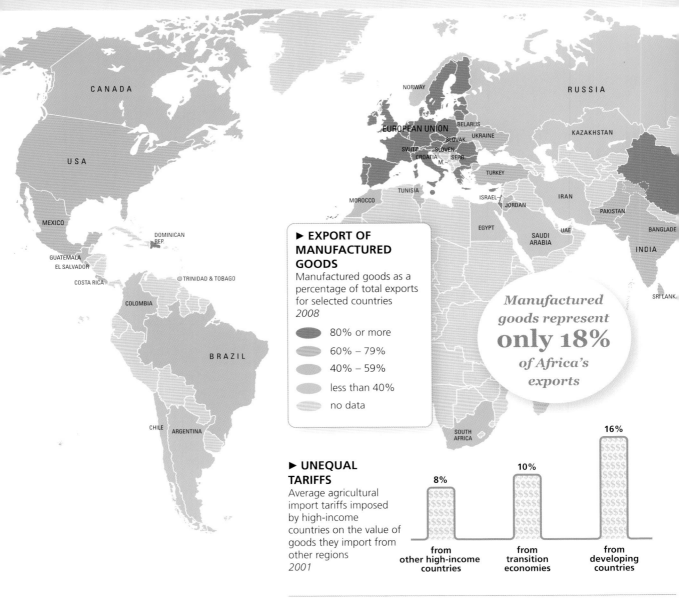

CANADA

USA

MEXICO

DOMINICAN REP.

GUATEMALA
EL SALVADOR

COSTA RICA

TRINIDAD & TOBAGO

COLOMBIA

BRAZIL

CHILE   ARGENTINA

NORWAY

RUSSIA

EUROPEAN UNION

BELARUS

KAZAKHSTAN

UKRAINE

SLOVAK.

SWITZ.   SLOVEN.
CROATIA   SERB.
M.–

TURKEY

IRAN

TUNISIA

MOROCCO

ISRAEL
JORDAN

EGYPT

SAUDI
ARABIA

UAE

PAKISTAN

BANGLADE

INDIA

SRI LANK.

SOUTH
AFRICA

▶ EXPORT OF MANUFACTURED GOODS

Manufactured goods as a percentage of total exports for selected countries
2008

- 80% or more
- 60% – 79%
- 40% – 59%
- less than 40%
- no data

Manufactured goods represent **only 18%** *of Africa's exports*

▶ UNEQUAL TARIFFS

Average agricultural import tariffs imposed by high-income countries on the value of goods they import from other regions
2001

8%

from other high-income countries

10%

from transition economies

16%

from developing countries

Rich countries spend:
$1 billion a day
in agriculture subsidies for their own farmers
$1 billion a year
in agricultural aid for poor countries

▶ International trade is a powerful factor in determining the extent to which poor countries are able to share equally in global prosperity. The benefits of trade are, however, unevenly distributed, partly because industrialized countries maintain trade barriers in the form of high tariffs against goods from poor countries while maintaining mutually favorable terms with other rich countries.

The percentage of total exports represented by manufactured goods is one indicator of prosperity. By this measure, countries in Sub-Saharan Africa and Latin America are falling behind. Although most industrial countries, including the USA, followed policies to protect their infant industries as they were industrializing, that route is now discouraged by international financial organizations, including the IMF and WTO, which promote free trade.

Globally determined commodity prices, and the high tariffs imposed by rich countries on imports from poorer nations, favor the rich and create barriers to trade equality.

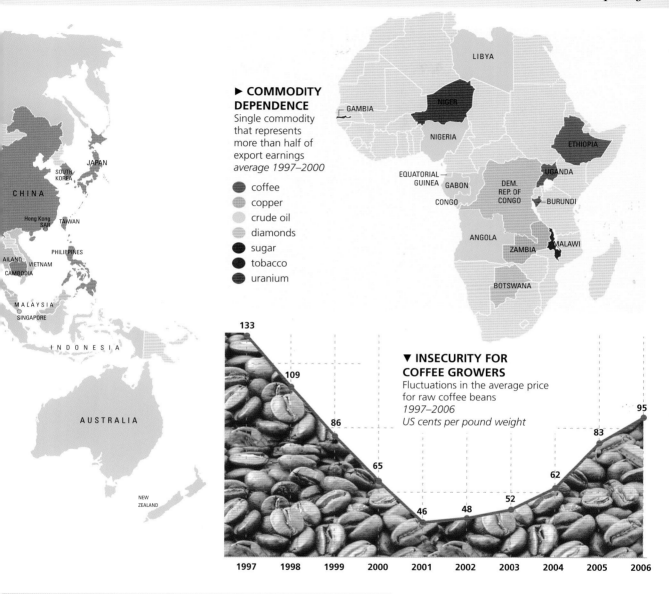

► COMMODITY DEPENDENCE
Single commodity that represents more than half of export earnings
average 1997–2000

- coffee
- copper
- crude oil
- diamonds
- sugar
- tobacco
- uranium

▼ INSECURITY FOR COFFEE GROWERS
Fluctuations in the average price for raw coffee beans
1997–2006
US cents per pound weight

133
109
86
65
46
48
52
62
83
95

1997 1998 1999 2000 2001 2002 2003 2004 2005 2006

This dissemination of global ideas in favor of free trade and against the protection of "infant industries" may have reduced the capacity of poorer economies to diversify and to promote industrial production. Some developing countries depend on a limited number of agricultural commodity exports, making them vulnerable to volatile and falling prices. Free trade ideas have done little, however, to restrain rich countries from subsidizing their own agricultural production, the surplus from which is "dumped" overseas, undercutting local producers.

Power is also exercised by rich countries through the imposition of rules on intellectual property rights, making the transfer of technology expensive for poor countries, and raising the price of medicines, which adversely affects the health of the poor.

Budget Priorities

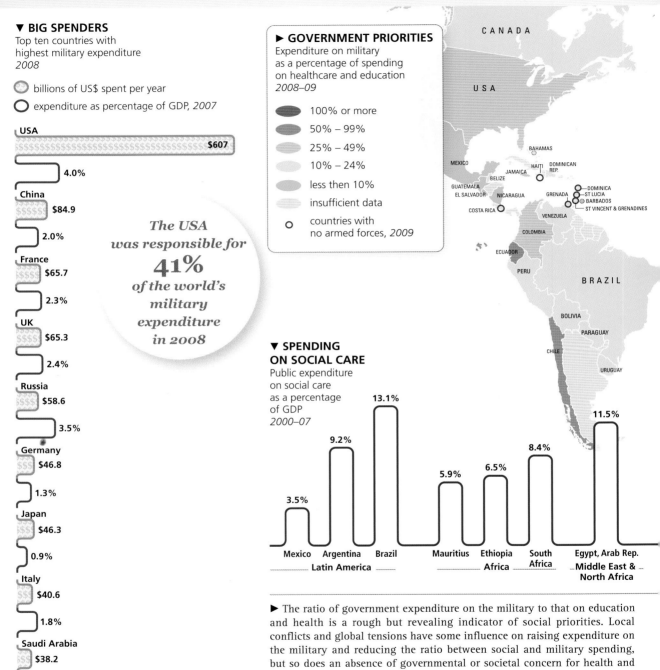

▼ BIG SPENDERS
Top ten countries with highest military expenditure
2008

- billions of US$ spent per year
- expenditure as percentage of GDP, *2007*

USA
$607
4.0%

China
$84.9
2.0%

France
$65.7
2.3%

UK
$65.3
2.4%

Russia
$58.6
3.5%

Germany
$46.8
1.3%

Japan
$46.3
0.9%

Italy
$40.6
1.8%

Saudi Arabia
$38.2
9.3%

India
$30.0
2.5%

The USA was responsible for **41%** *of the world's military expenditure in 2008*

► GOVERNMENT PRIORITIES
Expenditure on military as a percentage of spending on healthcare and education
2008–09

- 100% or more
- 50% – 99%
- 25% – 49%
- 10% – 24%
- less then 10%
- insufficient data
- countries with no armed forces, *2009*

▼ SPENDING ON SOCIAL CARE
Public expenditure on social care as a percentage of GDP
2000–07

Latin America			Africa		South Africa	Middle East & North Africa
Mexico	Argentina	Brazil	Mauritius	Ethiopia		Egypt, Arab Rep.
3.5%	9.2%	13.1%	5.9%	6.5%	8.4%	11.5%

► The ratio of government expenditure on the military to that on education and health is a rough but revealing indicator of social priorities. Local conflicts and global tensions have some influence on raising expenditure on the military and reducing the ratio between social and military spending, but so does an absence of governmental or societal concern for health and education.

A small number of mostly small states have managed without overt military forces. In many cases, these countries also have high levels of social spending, often with markedly positive impacts on reducing inequalities and improving well-being. Some states, such as Costa Rica, manage to combine high well-being with relatively low government spending and low economic growth.

The proportion of GDP that governments spend on the military, healthcare, education, and social security provides one measure of their social priorities.

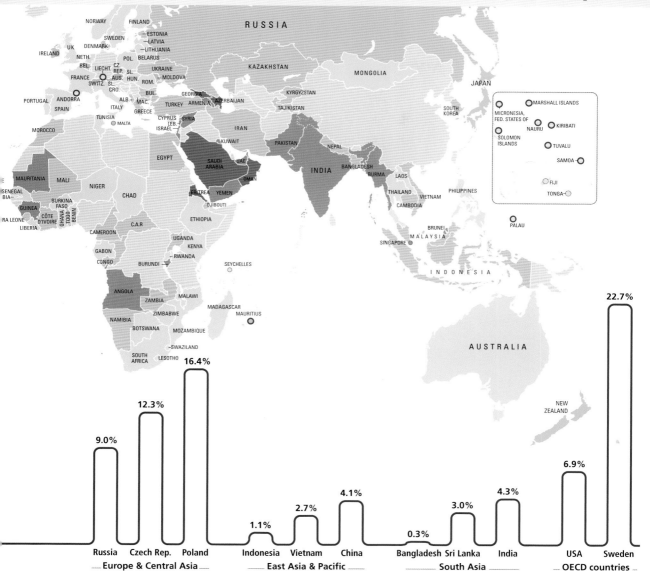

From the late 1970s, the rise of neo-liberalism, which seeks to minimize the role of the state and maximize the private business sector, encouraged governments across the globe to privatize state industries and reduce state spending. Healthcare, education and social security were disproportionately cut, while many states protected military spending. These ideas led to widespread austerity. An increase in inequalities followed, with women in many poor households taking on extra work to substitute for lost livelihoods, and to pay for education, health and social support.

Social spending is higher in industrial countries than in the developing world, but better basic safety nets could prevent illness and other personal disasters causing a rapid descent into poverty for those living on a financial knife edge.

Proportion of GDP spent on social support:
OECD countries:
more than
13%
Low-income countries:
less than
2%

Government Action

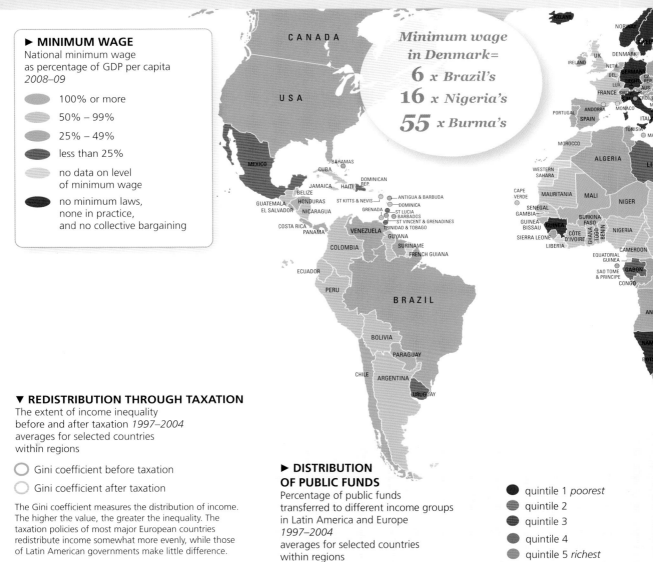

► MINIMUM WAGE
National minimum wage
as percentage of GDP per capita
2008–09

- 100% or more
- 50% – 99%
- 25% – 49%
- less than 25%
- no data on level of minimum wage
- no minimum laws, none in practice, and no collective bargaining

Minimum wage in Denmark=

6 *x Brazil's*

16 *x Nigeria's*

55 *x Burma's*

▼ REDISTRIBUTION THROUGH TAXATION
The extent of income inequality
before and after taxation *1997–2004*
averages for selected countries
within regions

- ◯ Gini coefficient before taxation
- ◯ Gini coefficient after taxation

The Gini coefficient measures the distribution of income. The higher the value, the greater the inequality. The taxation policies of most major European countries redistribute income somewhat more evenly, while those of Latin American governments make little difference.

Europe

45

31

Latin America

53

51

► DISTRIBUTION OF PUBLIC FUNDS
Percentage of public funds
transferred to different income groups
in Latin America and Europe
1997–2004
averages for selected countries
within regions

- ● quintile 1 *poorest*
- ● quintile 2
- ● quintile 3
- ● quintile 4
- ● quintile 5 *richest*

► Diverse forms of government action, from wage laws to taxation, and the provision of education and healthcare to the redistribution of land, seek to address inequality. Such actions from those in power are usually in response to pressures, representations and movements from, among others, workers, minorities, peasants and women. They include a range of measures, both coercive and persuasive.

Laws that set a minimum wage are one way of increasing the income of the poorest workers. They are likely to be more effective where people are formally employed in the industrialized sector, rather than in informal unregulated work and enterprise. Redistribution through progressive taxation, which taxes the better-off at a higher rate in order to reduce the tax burden on the poor, is used in many European countries, but is less

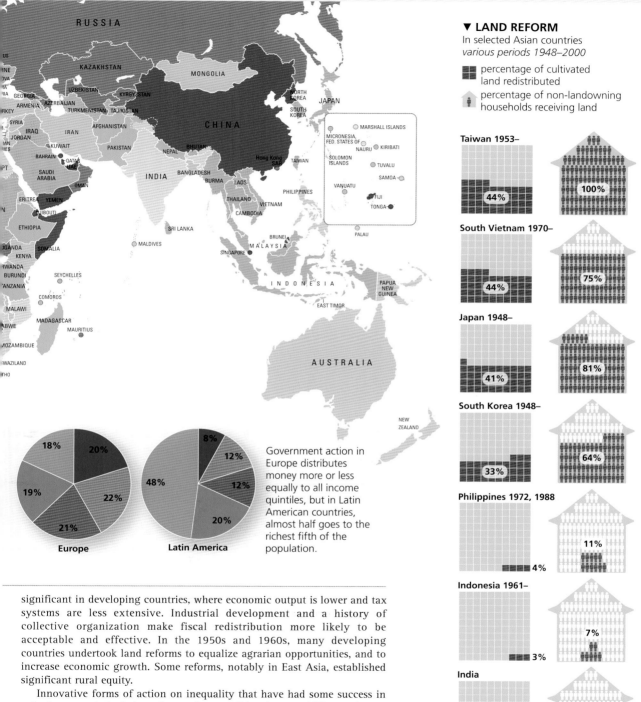

▼ LAND REFORM
In selected Asian countries
various periods 1948–2000

▨ percentage of cultivated land redistributed

👤 percentage of non-landowning households receiving land

Taiwan 1953–
44%   100%

South Vietnam 1970–
44%   75%

Japan 1948–
41%   81%

South Korea 1948–
33%   64%

Philippines 1972, 1988
4%   11%

Indonesia 1961–
3%   7%

India
1.2%   11%

18% 20%
19% 22%
21%

Europe

8%
12%
48% 12%
20%

Latin America

Government action in Europe distributes money more or less equally to all income quintiles, but in Latin American countries, almost half goes to the richest fifth of the population.

significant in developing countries, where economic output is lower and tax systems are less extensive. Industrial development and a history of collective organization make fiscal redistribution more likely to be acceptable and effective. In the 1950s and 1960s, many developing countries undertook land reforms to equalize agrarian opportunities, and to increase economic growth. Some reforms, notably in East Asia, established significant rural equity.

Innovative forms of action on inequality that have had some success in reducing poverty include cash transfers conditional upon children going to school. However, the way such policies are implemented, and lack of support at all levels of the economic and political order, may undo or reverse their effects.

Freedom & Democracy

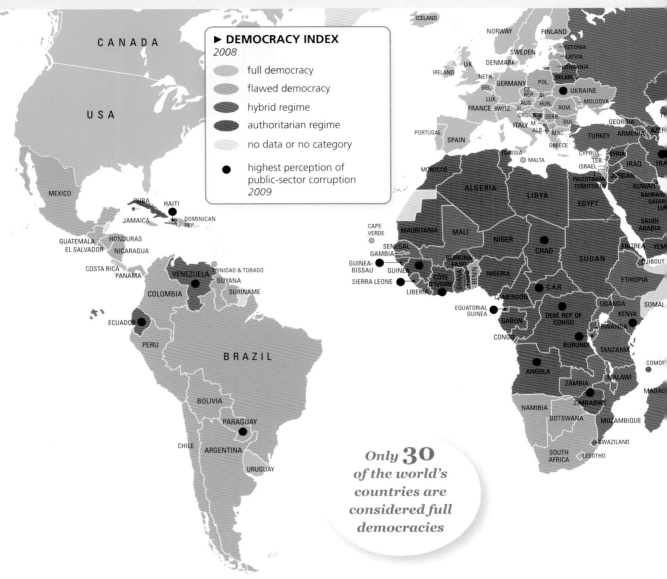

DEMOCRACY INDEX
2008

- full democracy
- flawed democracy
- hybrid regime
- authoritarian regime
- no data or no category
- ● highest perception of public-sector corruption *2009*

Only **30** *of the world's countries are considered full democracies*

The Economist Democracy Index

This assesses the extent to which states achieve democracy by measuring their performance in:

1. electoral process and pluralism
2. functioning of government
3. political participation
4. political culture
5. civil liberties

▶ Freedoms can be seen as both ends in themselves, and as means of achieving a fulfilled life. Democracy is a form of collective decision making in which participants are equal at some stage of the process, for example, when voting. Both freedom and democracy are complex, contested ideas which change over time, but even rough measures can provide an indication of significant inequalities between and within countries.

National democracies exist within complex global systems that are not democratic. Although the UN General Assembly uses a system of one-government one-vote, which is an indirect form of representation, the UN Security Council only represents leading governments and a few others, without any pretense of democracy. Other global actors, such as corporations, similarly lack democratic accountability.

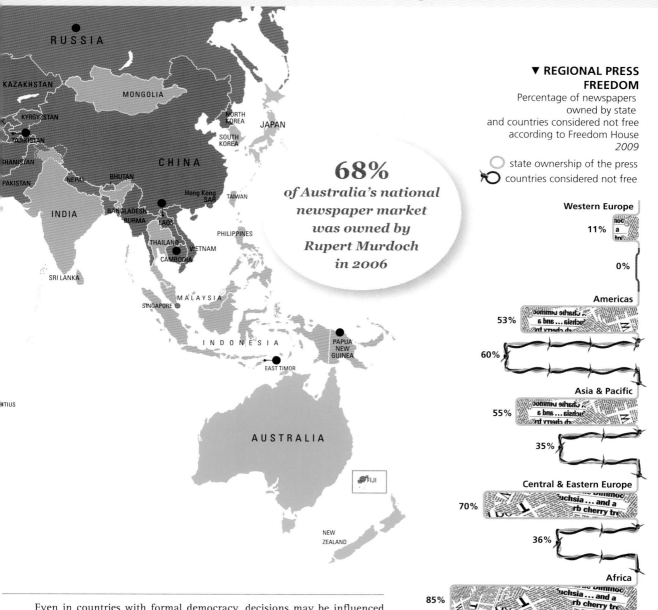

68% *of Australia's national newspaper market was owned by Rupert Murdoch in 2006*

▼ **REGIONAL PRESS FREEDOM**
Percentage of newspapers owned by state and countries considered not free according to Freedom House
2009

○ state ownership of the press
countries considered not free

Western Europe
11%
0%

Americas
53%
60%

Asia & Pacific
55%
35%

Central & Eastern Europe
70%
36%

Africa
85%
48%

Middle East & North Africa
94%
79%

Even in countries with formal democracy, decisions may be influenced by corruption (a diverse array of moral and legal offenses). The failure of governments to be accountable for their actions, or to allow citizens, particularly minority groups, an opportunity to express their views, is also a restriction on democratic freedom, which can actually alter the course of events, leading, for example, to the failure to prevent disasters such as famine.

The concentration of ownership of television and newspapers also influences how collective decision-making occurs. Neither government control nor concentrated private control provide freedom and accountability. It remains to be seen if the internet will generate sustainable alternatives in this arena.

Incarceration & Execution

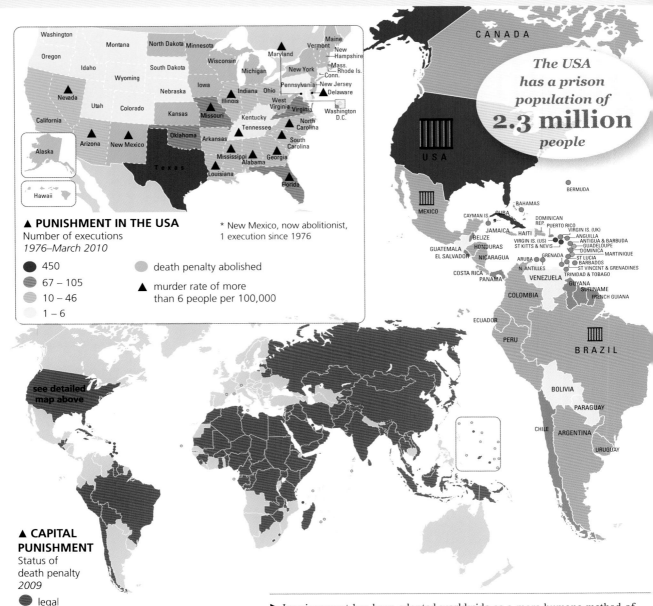

The USA has a prison population of **2.3 million** people

▲ PUNISHMENT IN THE USA
Number of executions
1976–March 2010

* New Mexico, now abolitionist, 1 execution since 1976

- ● 450
- ● 67 – 105
- ● 10 – 46
- ● 1 – 6

- ● death penalty abolished

- ▲ murder rate of more than 6 people per 100,000

▲ CAPITAL PUNISHMENT
Status of death penalty *2009*

- ● legal
- ● not legal

see detailed map above

▶ Imprisonment has been adopted worldwide as a more humane method of control than older, more barbaric, punishments. However, the extent to which it is used, and the philosophy underlying it, vary widely. The USA is one of the most enthusiastic jailors, with 0.75 percent of its population behind bars. This comes at a cost. In California, in 2010, almost 11 percent of spending went to prisons and only 7.5 percent to higher education.

The death penalty is perhaps the most irreparable of inequalities because a life lost cannot be regained. Since 1973, more than 139 people have been released from death rows in the USA alone due to evidence that they were wrongfully convicted.

While 95 countries have abolished the death penalty for all crimes, over 100 countries have retained it, although 44 of those reserve it for special

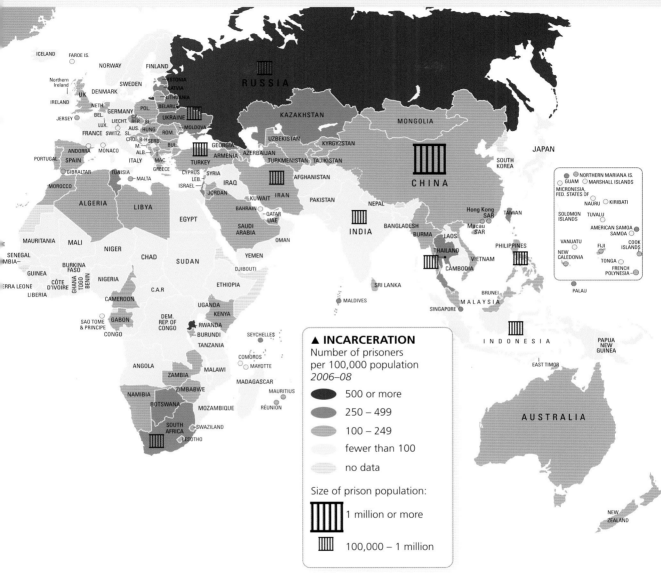

▲ INCARCERATION

Number of prisoners per 100,000 population
2006–08

- 500 or more
- 250 – 499
- 100 – 249
- fewer than 100
- no data

Size of prison population:

- 1 million or more
- 100,000 – 1 million

circumstances. In 2008, more than 70 percent of known executions took place in China.

In the USA, the death penalty is carried out most often on the poor partly because few on death row can afford effective representation. And it is most likely to be used to punish murderers of white victims. This was the case for 79 percent of executions between 1977 and 2008, even though about half of all homicide victims were African-Americans. Between 1976 and 2010, the homicide rate in states with the death penalty was 5.2 people per 100,000, which was higher than in states without the death penalty, where it was 3.3.

40%
of the world's prisoners are in China and the USA

▼ ECONOMIC VULNERABILITY

Percentage of lower- and
upper-class households
experiencing different levels of
economic vulnerability
1994–98

 no economic vulnerability

transient economic vulnerability

recurrent economic vulnerability

persistent economic vulnerability

lower class – people working in services, sales,
clerical, and lower technical occupations
upper class – people working in higher grade
professional, administrative, and managerial
occupations, and employers
economic vulnerability – when households
are unable to afford capabilities such as heating
their home, buying new clothes and having an
annual holiday, or unable to own or access
goods such as a car, TV, or telephone

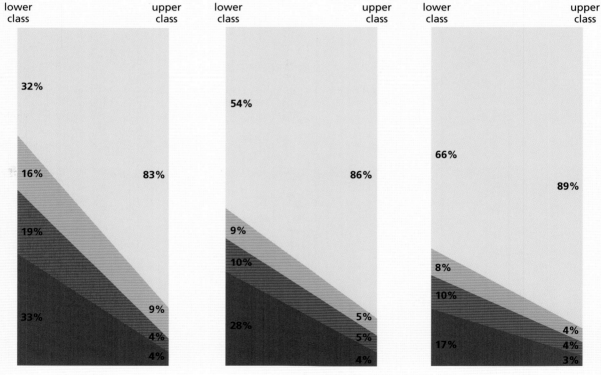

lower class	upper class
32%	
16%	83%
19%	
33%	9%
	4%
	4%

Greece

lower class	upper class
54%	
9%	86%
10%	
28%	5%
	5%
	4%

Italy

lower class	upper class
66%	
	89%
8%	
10%	
17%	4%
	4%
	3%

Netherlands

Social Inequalities   3

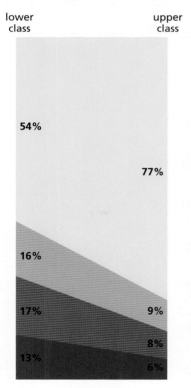

lower class   upper class

54%

77%

16%

17%   9%

8%

13%   6%

Denmark

► Social inequalities are differences in human interactions, groups and institutions that are generated by a process of differentiation and domination, often built upon visible distinctions between one group and another. Frequently, biological cues such as skin color, sex, or appearance, are used as the basis for constructing ideas of difference. Then, exclusion from areas of work or social life, or differential pay rates, may be used to establish a pattern of domination. By this method one group establishes preferential conditions and dominates another. This is what happens with race and ethnicity, sex and gender, class, and age.

These axes of inequality are used in all societies, sometimes with other differences, such as disability, language, and sexual orientation, to exclude some and benefit others. The practice of differentiation and domination influences social relationships, institutions, groups and much else. When biological cues are involved, it is common for difference and inequality to be naturalized in some way, such as the exclusion of women from certain occupations on the grounds of physical weakness. While biological differences can matter in some situations, broad claims based on nature, such as "women's place is in the home" frequently hide a long history of domination by the group, in this case men, propagating the claim.

People in a lower class experience economic vulnerability with greater frequency than those in a higher class, as shown in the graphic. This can, however, be reduced by governments, such as those of Denmark and the Netherlands, providing more effective protection for those in lower-class service and clerical occupations.

Dimensions of inequality – race, class and gender – interact with one another. So, poor peasant women in many parts of the world are subject to additive inequalities due to their class position and their gender. Minorities who are also working class or poor are subject to inequalities resulting from their economic status and appearance or ethnicity.

In times of social crisis, such as economic recession and conquest through imperial expansion, domination along lines of difference may be particularly marked. Minorities may be targeted for unemployment during economic recessions. New ideas of subjection, and more virulent forms of racism may be generated to justify colonial expansion.

Social inequalities are experienced as a denial of freedoms and of respect. In response, some excluded groups establish collective identities and movements that open up previously excluded capabilities. Movements for national independence, for civil rights in the USA, and the gay and feminist movements wordwide, may provide examples for this process of struggle and empowerment.

Gender

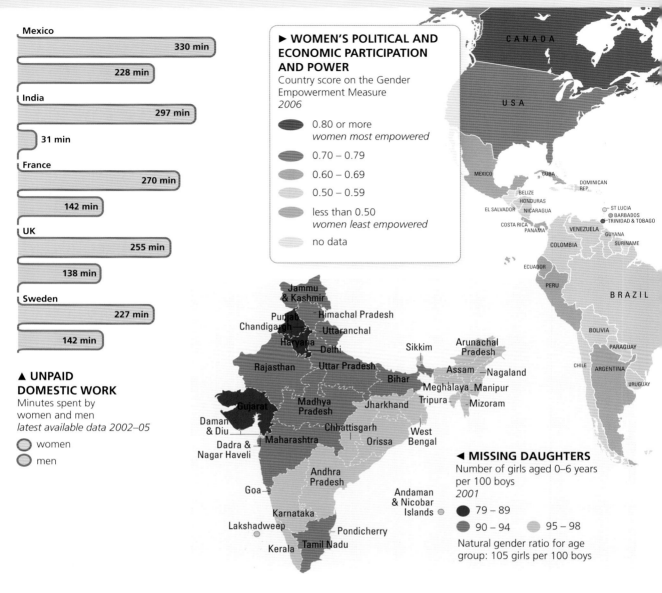

Mexico
330 min
228 min

India
297 min
31 min

France
270 min
142 min

UK
255 min
138 min

Sweden
227 min
142 min

▲ **UNPAID DOMESTIC WORK**
Minutes spent by women and men
latest available data 2002–05
○ women
○ men

► **WOMEN'S POLITICAL AND ECONOMIC PARTICIPATION AND POWER**
Country score on the Gender Empowerment Measure
2006

- 0.80 or more *women most empowered*
- 0.70 – 0.79
- 0.60 – 0.69
- 0.50 – 0.59
- less than 0.50 *women least empowered*
- no data

◄ **MISSING DAUGHTERS**
Number of girls aged 0–6 years per 100 boys
2001
- 79 – 89
- 90 – 94
- 95 – 98

Natural gender ratio for age group: 105 girls per 100 boys

Women in India spend

9 times

the hours of men on domestic work

► Gender subordination, or bias against women, is the most widespread and longest standing inequality. Sexual divisions are a basis for understanding a society. Even in matriarchal societies, men usually have more influence than women. Gender inequalities are pervasive in social practices and institutions, from language and gesture to hospitals and legislatures.

Gender inequalities are difficult to capture in one measure. One gauge of the extent of women's representation is the Gender Empowerment Measure which combines three indices – of political representation, position in influential jobs, and power over economic resources.

While gender subordination is thought to be universal, the forms it takes vary. The most dramatic example relates to "son preference" in a belt of societies from North Africa, through South Asia to China. Because of this

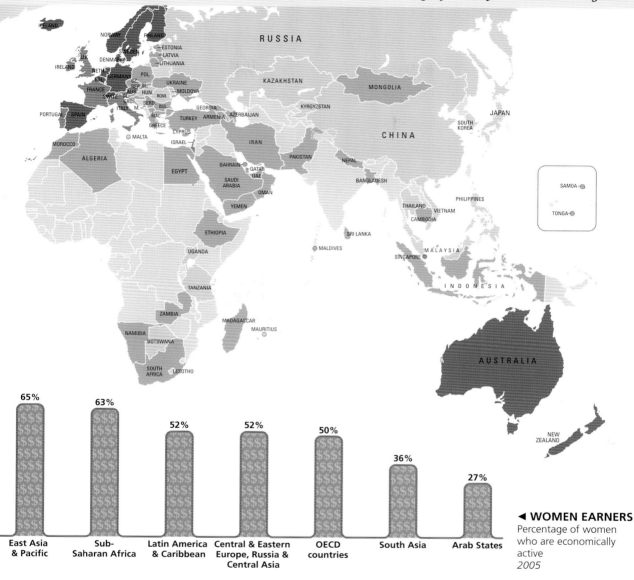

◀ WOMEN EARNERS
Percentage of women who are economically active
2005

bias, more than 100 million fewer girl babies than would be expected are born and grow to adulthood. Many girls die because their families are less likely to seek healthcare for them than for their sons. Some die through infanticide. And, with the increasing availability of fetal sex identification, many girl babies are aborted.

In most societies, long-standing divisions of work allocate most home-based work, including fuel and water collection, childcare, cooking, and healthcare, to women. These home-based tasks combine with paid work to give many women longer working hours than men. Nonetheless, participation in paid work outside the home, even though women are paid less than men, does provide women with greater influence. There is clear scope for reforming the gender division of labor.

In China in 2007 for every
100 boys
aged 0–4 years there were only
80 girls

Age

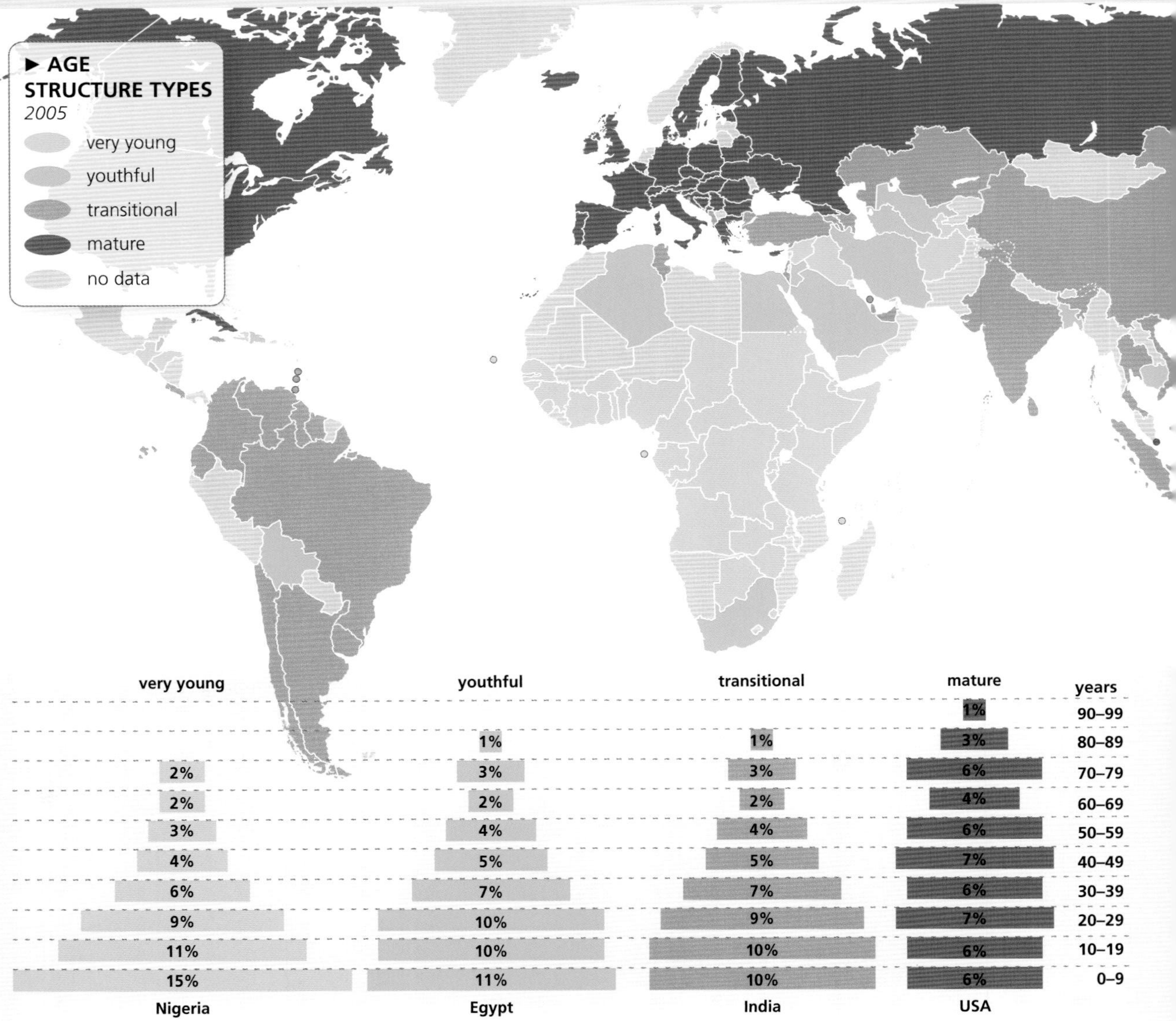

► AGE STRUCTURE TYPES
2005

- very young
- youthful
- transitional
- mature
- no data

very young	youthful	transitional	mature	years
			1%	90–99
	1%	1%	3%	80–89
2%	3%	3%	6%	70–79
2%	2%	2%	4%	60–69
3%	4%	4%	6%	50–59
4%	5%	5%	7%	40–49
6%	7%	7%	6%	30–39
9%	10%	9%	7%	20–29
11%	10%	10%	6%	10–19
15%	11%	10%	6%	0–9
Nigeria	**Egypt**	**India**	**USA**	

By 2050
90%
of people aged 15 to 24 will be living in developing countries

► Inequalities of age have some similarities to those of gender, race and class. All four operate through processes of differentiation and domination. As with gender subordination, age inequalities are reproduced through exclusion, and through devaluing the work and contributions of a particular group. The productive capacity of the younger generation is predicated on the work and investment of the generation that went before, but this may not be recognized in pension or social security payments. The four axes of inequality – class, gender, race and age – also interact. Thus, elderly women in certain minorities and the working class are most at risk of poverty.

Population pyramids reveal contrasting age structures between nations. Some have mostly young people. Others have a substantial number of old people. These patterns are sometimes used to support apocalyptic narratives

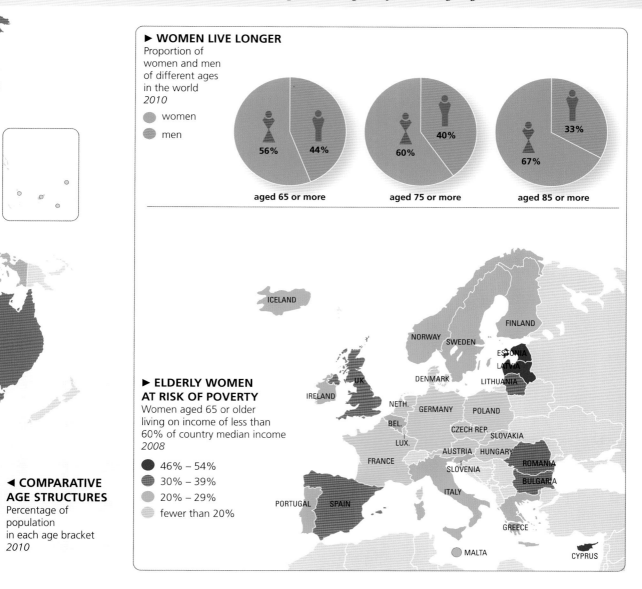

► **WOMEN LIVE LONGER**
Proportion of women and men of different ages in the world
2010

● women
● men

56%   44%
aged 65 or more

60%   40%
aged 75 or more

67%   33%
aged 85 or more

◄ **COMPARATIVE AGE STRUCTURES**
Percentage of population in each age bracket
2010

► **ELDERLY WOMEN AT RISK OF POVERTY**
Women aged 65 or older living on income of less than 60% of country median income
2008

● 46% – 54%
● 30% – 39%
● 20% – 29%
● fewer than 20%

ICELAND NORWAY SWEDEN FINLAND ESTONIA LATVIA
UK DENMARK LITHUANIA
IRELAND NETH. GERMANY POLAND
BEL. CZECH REP. SLOVAKIA
LUX. AUSTRIA HUNGARY
FRANCE SLOVENIA ROMANIA
BULGARIA
ITALY
PORTUGAL SPAIN
GREECE
MALTA CYPRUS

of unemployment and the rise of unrest in the youthful regions, and of gerontocracy and the collapse of pensions in the older regions.

These nationalist narratives can be transcended with a global perspective. National demographic charts assume that there is no migration, and that cross-border economic transactions are insignificant. Of course, such transactions are steadily increasing, and migration to find work is a long-standing feature of the global economy. Recognition of these global processes undermines the apocalyptic myths, and suggests ways of responding practically to demographic differences.

If restrictions on economic migrants can be relaxed, the fear of populations burdened with pension payments and less productive people can be dispelled.

Class

Different ways of defining class	Assets and resources on which stratification depends
Economic	Ownership of land, farms, factories, professional practices, businesses, liquid assets, humans (slaves), labor power (serfs)
Political	Household authority, workplace authority, party and social authority (e.g. legislator)
Cultural	Consumption practices, "manners", lifestyle
Social	Status of social networks, social ties, associations and clubs
Honorific	Level of prestige, reputation, fame, deference and derogation, ethnic and religious purity
Civil	Rights of property, contract, franchise, and membership of elective assemblies
Human	Skills, expertise, experience, formal education, knowledge

► OWNER–EMPLOYEE RELATIONSHIP

Percentage of population in each class
in selected industrialized countries
1997

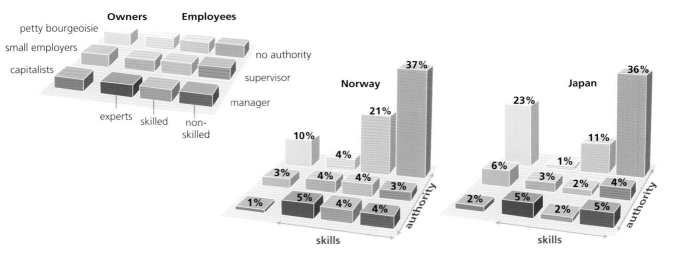

> "Class is a group whose members share a common economic position, differentiated in terms of power and status, and the chances of bettering themselves in material terms."
> **Harriett Bradley, 1996**

► One of the most influential ways of depicting multidimensional inequalities comes from analysis of social class. Inequalities of economic opportunity, power and status correspond closely with class divisions. Particular class relationships have been characteristic of different historical eras. Thus, land formed the basis for political power in medieval Europe. A land-holding aristocracy dominated serfs, who provided free labor or produce in return for use of the land.

In contemporary societies, under the economic order of industrial capitalism, those who own productive assets, factories, land, and companies have an unrivaled capacity to accumulate wealth. This wealth, in turn, can be translated into political power and social influence. At the other end of

Class divisions separate the rich and powerful from those who have little opportunity to gain wealth and influence.

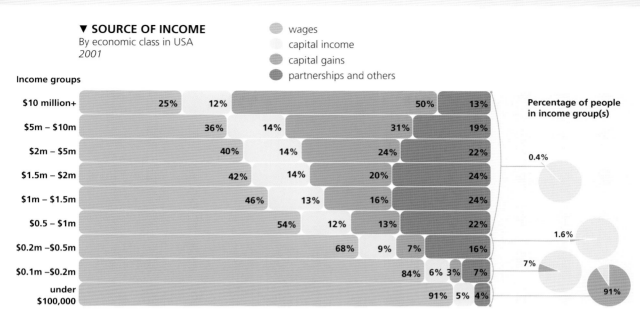

▼ SOURCE OF INCOME
By economic class in USA
2001

- wages
- capital income
- capital gains
- partnerships and others

Income groups

$10 million+	25%	12%	50% 13%
$5m – $10m	36%	14%	31% 19%
$2m – $5m	40%	14%	24% 22%
$1.5m – $2m	42%	14%	20% 24%
$1m – $1.5m	46%	13%	16% 24%
$0.5 – $1m	54%	12%	13% 22%
$0.2m –$0.5m	68%	9%	7% 16%
$0.1m –$0.2m	84%	6% 3%	7%
under $100,000	91%	5% 4%	

Percentage of people in income group(s)

0.4%

1.6%

7%

91%

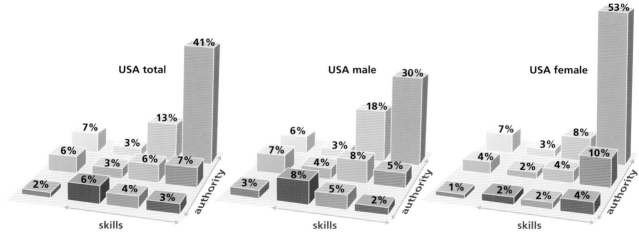

USA total
41% 13% 7% 3% 6% 3% 6% 6% 2% 4% 3%
skills / authority

USA male
30% 18% 6% 3% 7% 4% 8% 5% 3% 8% 5% 2%
skills / authority

USA female
53% 8% 7% 3% 4% 10% 4% 2% 4% 1% 2% 2%
skills / authority

the social scale, those who are employed in factories, companies, or farms as workers have little ability to accumulate wealth, and generally little power. In fact, the ability of the owners of companies to accumulate is in part related to their ability to limit the incomes of their workers. This explains a fundamental inequality of contemporary capitalism.

Contemporary forms of class and economic inequality relate also to authority and skill. It is not just company owners who can accumulate, but also senior managers and financiers, and those with professional skills, such as medical training, who may be able to demand large salaries.

Data are rarely collected about social class. Few governments acknowledge such profound, durable and multi-dimensional inequalities.

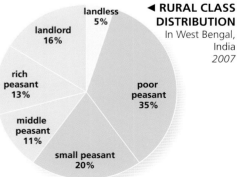

◄ RURAL CLASS DISTRIBUTION
In West Bengal, India
2007

- landless 5%
- landlord 16%
- rich peasant 13%
- middle peasant 11%
- small peasant 20%
- poor peasant 35%

Race & Ethnicity

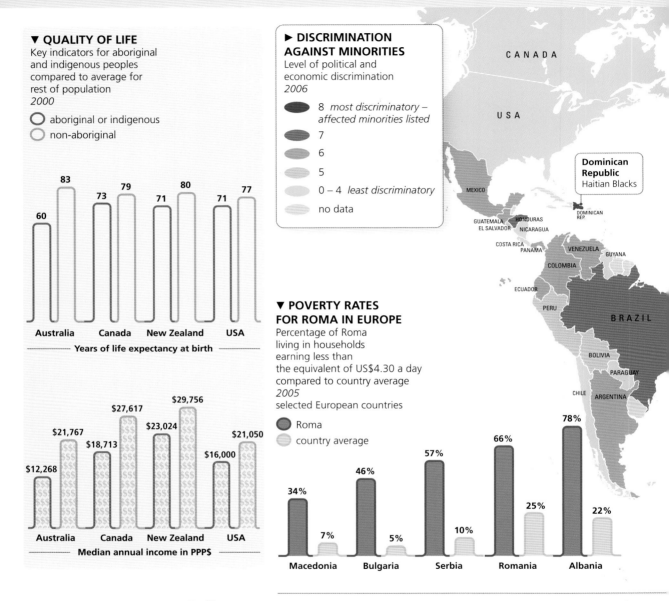

▼ QUALITY OF LIFE

Key indicators for aboriginal and indigenous peoples compared to average for rest of population
2000

○ aboriginal or indigenous
○ non-aboriginal

Years of life expectancy at birth

	Australia	Canada	New Zealand	USA
aboriginal	60	73	71	71
non-aboriginal	83	79	80	77

Median annual income in PPP$

	Australia	Canada	New Zealand	USA
aboriginal	$12,268	$18,713	$23,024	$16,000
non-aboriginal	$21,767	$27,617	$29,756	$21,050

► DISCRIMINATION AGAINST MINORITIES

Level of political and economic discrimination
2006

- 8 *most discriminatory – affected minorities listed*
- 7
- 6
- 5
- 0 – 4 *least discriminatory*
- no data

Dominican Republic
Haitian Blacks

▼ POVERTY RATES FOR ROMA IN EUROPE

Percentage of Roma living in households earning less than the equivalent of US$4.30 a day compared to country average
2005
selected European countries

● Roma
○ country average

	Macedonia	Bulgaria	Serbia	Romania	Albania
Roma	34%	46%	57%	66%	78%
country average	7%	5%	10%	25%	22%

Indigenous peoples:
5%
of the world's population
15%
of the world's poor

► People want the freedom to practice their religion openly, to speak their own language, and to celebrate their racial or ethnic heritage without prejudice or diminished opportunity. There are more than 5,000 ethnic groups, 4,000 faiths, and 9,000 languages in the world. Membership of minority groups is primarily determined by descent, and many have distinguishing physical characteristics, or a common language, religion, or customs. Many minority groups suffer systematic or institutionalized exclusion from political, economic, and social opportunities. Many are alternatively or additionally denied recognition and accommodation of their ways of life.

Most aboriginal peoples are victims of a long history of colonization and oppression, dispossession of land, loss of resources, language, and the

Some minority ethnic and religious groups suffer systematic discrimination. Inequalities associated with ethnicity are frequently intertwined with those of gender and poverty.

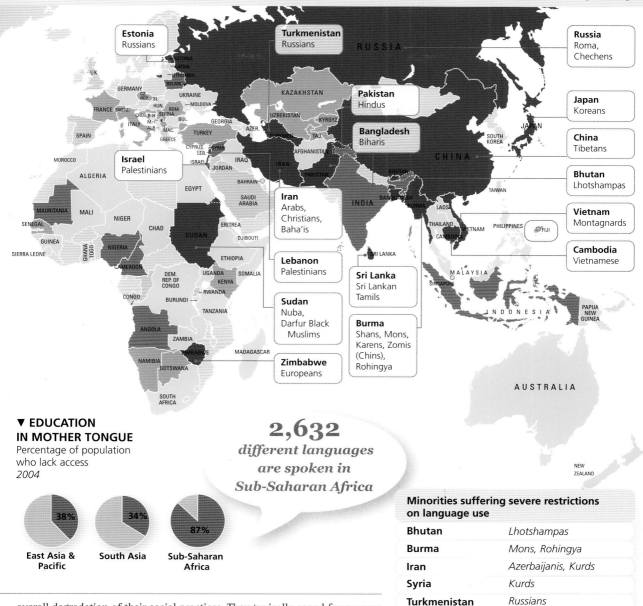

Estonia Russians

Turkmenistan Russians

Russia Roma, Chechens

Pakistan Hindus

Japan Koreans

Bangladesh Biharis

China Tibetans

Israel Palestinians

Bhutan Lhotshampas

Iran Arabs, Christians, Baha'is

Vietnam Montagnards

Lebanon Palestinians

Cambodia Vietnamese

Sri Lanka Sri Lankan Tamils

Sudan Nuba, Darfur Black Muslims

Burma Shans, Mons, Karens, Zomis (Chins), Rohingya

Zimbabwe Europeans

2,632 different languages are spoken in Sub-Saharan Africa

▼ EDUCATION IN MOTHER TONGUE
Percentage of population who lack access
2004

38% East Asia & Pacific

34% South Asia

87% Sub-Saharan Africa

Minorities suffering severe restrictions on language use	
Bhutan	*Lhotshampas*
Burma	*Mons, Rohingya*
Iran	*Azerbaijanis, Kurds*
Syria	*Kurds*
Turkmenistan	*Russians*

Minorities suffering severe restrictions on religious practice	
Burma	*Zomis (Chins), Rohingya*
China	*Tibetans, Turkmen*
Iran	*Baha'is*
Pakistan	*Ahmadis*
Saudi Arabia	*Shiites*
Vietnam	*Montagnards*

overall degradation of their social practices. They typically spend fewer years attending school and leave with lower achievements than their majority counterparts, with the result that many are poor, illiterate, and unemployed. But the problem is not confined to aboriginal populations. In the USA, three times as many blacks live in poverty as whites; Hispanics are imprisoned at 2.5 times, and African-Americans at 6.5 times the rate of whites.

Surveys suggest that multiple identities are common and that diversity has benefits. In Spain, for example, almost all citizens say they consider themselves Spanish as well as Catalan or Basque. There is a wide consensus that cultural differences alone are not causes of conflict but that economic and political inequalities over land, and other economic assets and lack of cultural recognition may contribute to tensions.

Child Labor

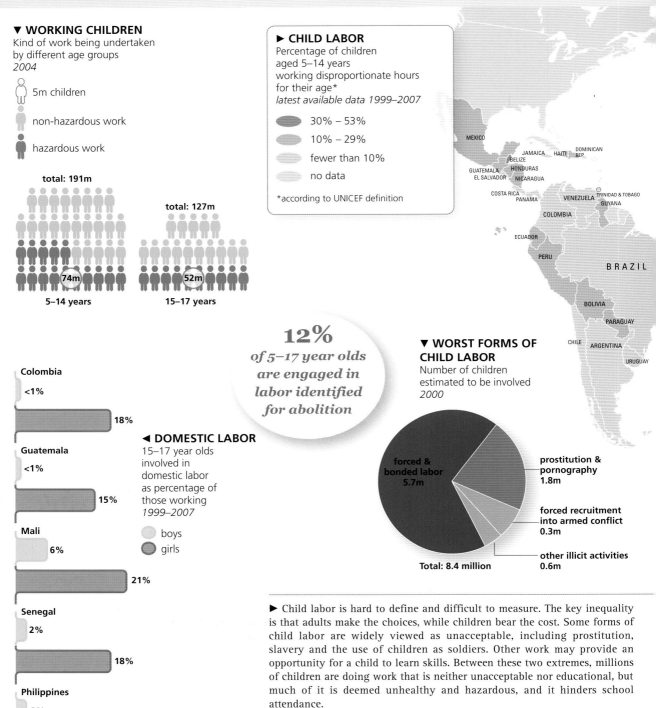

▼ WORKING CHILDREN
Kind of work being undertaken
by different age groups
2004

- 5m children
- non-hazardous work
- hazardous work

total: 191m

74m

5–14 years

total: 127m

52m

15–17 years

► CHILD LABOR
Percentage of children
aged 5–14 years
working disproportionate hours
for their age*
latest available data 1999–2007

- 30% – 53%
- 10% – 29%
- fewer than 10%
- no data

*according to UNICEF definition

MEXICO
JAMAICA   HAITI   DOMINICAN
BELIZE   REP.
GUATEMALA   HONDURAS
EL SALVADOR   NICARAGUA
COSTA RICA   VENEZUELA   TRINIDAD & TOBAGO
PANAMA   GUYANA
COLOMBIA
ECUADOR
PERU   B R A Z I L
BOLIVIA
PARAGUAY
CHILE   ARGENTINA
URUGUAY

12%
*of 5–17 year olds
are engaged in
labor identified
for abolition*

◄ DOMESTIC LABOR
15–17 year olds
involved in
domestic labor
as percentage of
those working
1999–2007

- boys
- girls

Colombia
<1%
18%

Guatemala
<1%
15%

Mali
6%
21%

Senegal
2%
18%

Philippines
2%
23%

▼ WORST FORMS OF CHILD LABOR
Number of children
estimated to be involved
2000

forced &
bonded labor
5.7m

prostitution &
pornography
1.8m

forced recruitment
into armed conflict
0.3m

other illicit activities
0.6m

Total: 8.4 million

► Child labor is hard to define and difficult to measure. The key inequality is that adults make the choices, while children bear the cost. Some forms of child labor are widely viewed as unacceptable, including prostitution, slavery and the use of children as soldiers. Other work may provide an opportunity for a child to learn skills. Between these two extremes, millions of children are doing work that is neither unacceptable nor educational, but much of it is deemed unhealthy and hazardous, and it hinders school attendance.

Between 180 million and 400 million children do more than 14 hours of paid work a week, or 28 hours of domestic work. Estimates suggest only a small proportion of them work in the most morally objectionable work, but that maybe half work in hazardous conditions.

Although child labor is decreasing, millions of children are employed in paid or household work. Raising wages and reducing poverty is the most effective way of reducing child labor.

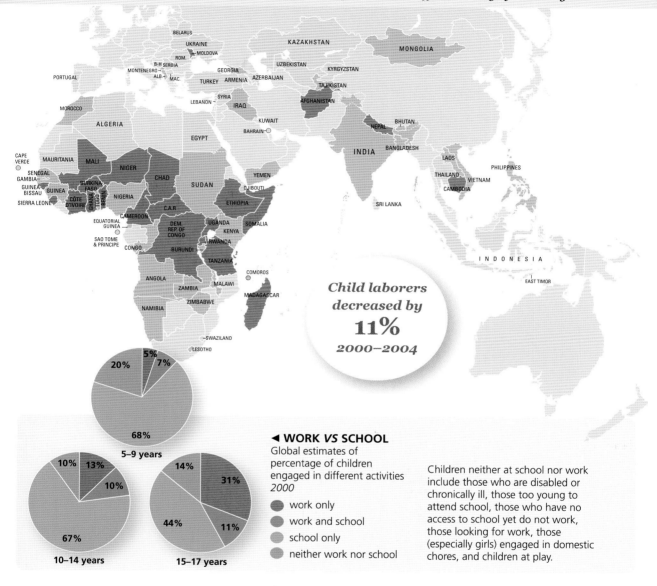

Child laborers decreased by **11%** 2000–2004

◀ WORK *VS* SCHOOL
Global estimates of percentage of children engaged in different activities *2000*

- work only
- work and school
- school only
- neither work nor school

5–9 years: 5%, 7%, 20%, 68%

10–14 years: 10%, 13%, 10%, 67%

15–17 years: 14%, 31%, 11%, 44%

Children neither at school nor work include those who are disabled or chronically ill, those too young to attend school, those who have no access to school yet do not work, those looking for work, those (especially girls) engaged in domestic chores, and children at play.

Although child labor in the developing world is less prevalent than during the process of industrialization in the western world in the 18th and 19th centuries, children's income is still vitally important for some poor families. A child from an orphaned, fatherless or large family, and those living on the street, are particularly vulnerable. Their parents or relative may be offered a loan, to be paid off by the child's labor, which results in the child spending years as a bonded laborer, little better off than a slave.

Coercive measures, such as child labor prohibitions backed by trade sanctions, may make families worse off, and drive children into more dangerous work, such as prostitution. Raising wages for adult employment, reducing unemployment, and rewarding children who go to school with money and work, reduces child labor.

25% *of economically active 5–14 year olds are in Sub-Saharan Africa;* **65%** *are in Asia & Pacific*

▼ PEOPLE LIVING IN POVERTY

Number of people living below $1.25 a day
1981–2005
by region

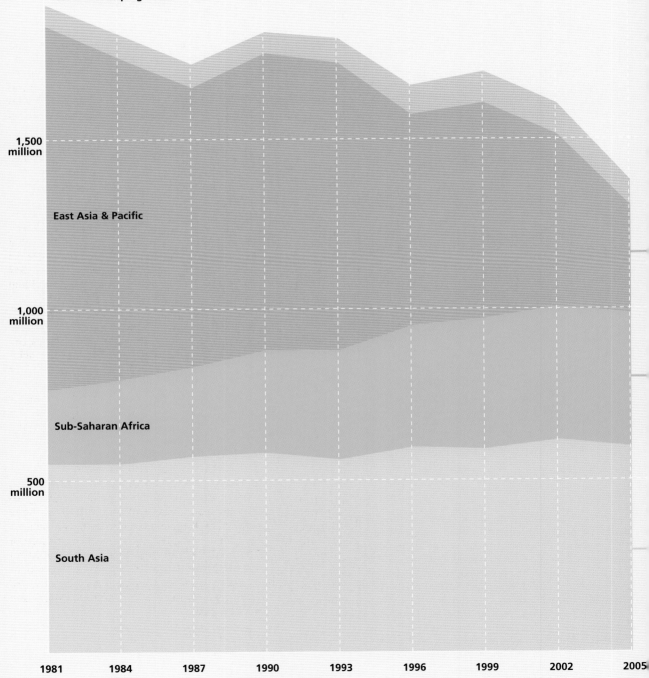

2,000 million

rest of developing world

1,500 million

East Asia & Pacific

1,000 million

Sub-Saharan Africa

500 million

South Asia

1981　1984　1987　1990　1993　1996　1999　2002　2005

▼ DEPTH OF POVERTY
Number of people in each region
living on different daily incomes
2005

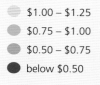

$1.00 – $1.25
$0.75 – $1.00
$0.50 – $0.75
below $0.50

▶ One way of thinking about poverty is as a situation in which people are excluded from the lives they would like to lead. More specifically, *income* poverty results in people being unable to afford the goods and services that might enable them to attain many of their aspirations.

This exclusion is illustrated by the response of rural Kenyans asked in a recent investigation what the poorest households would do with a small amount of additional money. First, they would buy food. With a little more money, their next priority would be to thatch their roof. After that, they would pay for primary education for children, then the purchase of chickens and goats. People who were able to get all those things, said these rural Kenyans, were no longer poor.

Although the proportion of the global population living in poverty is falling, even with the continuation of current trends, more than 1.3 billion people will still be living on less than $1.25 a day, and 2.6 billion people on less than $2.00 a day, in 2015.

This section explores poverty and inequalities in terms of access to basic capabilities that people need in order to live – food, water, energy, fuel, mobility, communications. Exclusion from these and many other capabilities or freedoms constitutes part of the wide aggregate of deprivations that contribute to the experience of poverty. As with income poverty, to which these inequalities contribute, differences of access have complex origins in individual circumstances, social relationships and physical infrastructures.

Thus, for example, access to safe and sufficient household water requires three things: i) the physical infrastructure delivering water, usually a network of pipes, pumps, storage and filtration, ii) the institutions to run that technological network, and iii) the social relationships (contracts, money, permits) giving an individual or household the ability to draw water from the network. Access to food and other essential needs such as energy, fuel, transport, or communications, similarly requires physical and social infrastructures for production and delivery of these services, and social relationships that give individual households entitlement to these services in the system.

The very poorest individuals tend to be from socially excluded groups, to live in remote areas with little education and few assets, or, in Asia, to be landless. The poorest households are likely to have experienced severe ill health, death of an adult, or to have suffered from conflict or an environmental shock such as drought.

Reductions in poverty have historically come about through some combination of industrialization and collective organization to support the living conditions of the poor. International agencies currently suggest that the poorest will be best served by targeted government action to support nutrition, health, and education, and to address the causes of social exclusion.

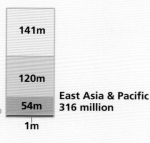

141m
120m
54m
1m

**East Asia & Pacific
316 million**

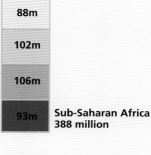

88m
102m
106m
93m

**Sub-Saharan Africa
388 million**

246m
229m
109m
12m

**South Asia
596 million**

Poverty

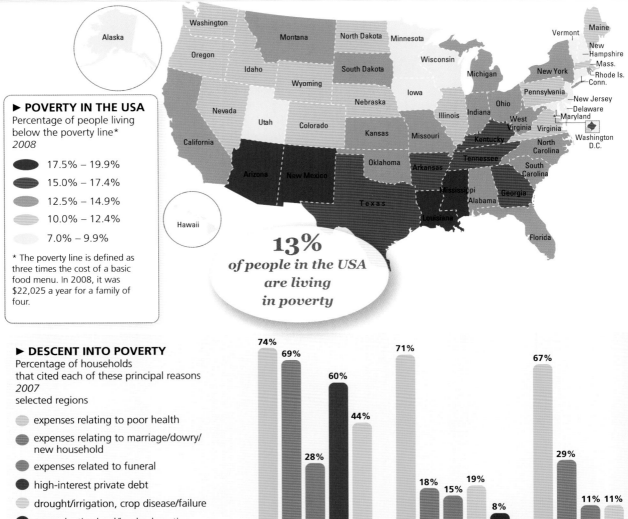

▶ POVERTY IN THE USA
Percentage of people living below the poverty line*
2008

- 17.5 – 19.9%
- 15.0 – 17.4%
- 12.5 – 14.9%
- 10.0 – 12.4%
- 7.0 – 9.9%

* The poverty line is defined as three times the cost of a basic food menu. In 2008, it was $22,025 a year for a family of four.

13% *of people in the USA are living in poverty*

▶ DESCENT INTO POVERTY
Percentage of households that cited each of these principal reasons
2007
selected regions

- expenses relating to poor health
- expenses relating to marriage/dowry/ new household
- expenses related to funeral
- high-interest private debt
- drought/irrigation, crop disease/failure
- unproductive land/land exhaustion

Andhra, India
74% 69% 28% 60% 44%

Uganda, Central & Western
71% 18% 15% 19% 8%

Peru, Puno, & Cajamarca
67% 29% 11% 11%

1 in 20 *people in the USA is living* **50%** *below the official poverty line*

▶ The disparity between rich and poor is one of the most widely recognized inequalities. Poverty can be seen simply as having little income, and few material possessions, but there have been recent conceptual and empirical advances in the understanding of the condition.

It is now recognized that an exclusive focus on income is inadequate and that poverty is multidimensional. It reflects vulnerability and limited autonomy, as well as material deprivation. What matters is whether people have the capability to lead the lives they aspire to. There is also new evidence about the immediate causes of descent into, and escape from, poverty.

Data on poverty generally reflect the simplest definition. Thus, most measures estimate the proportion of the population whose income or

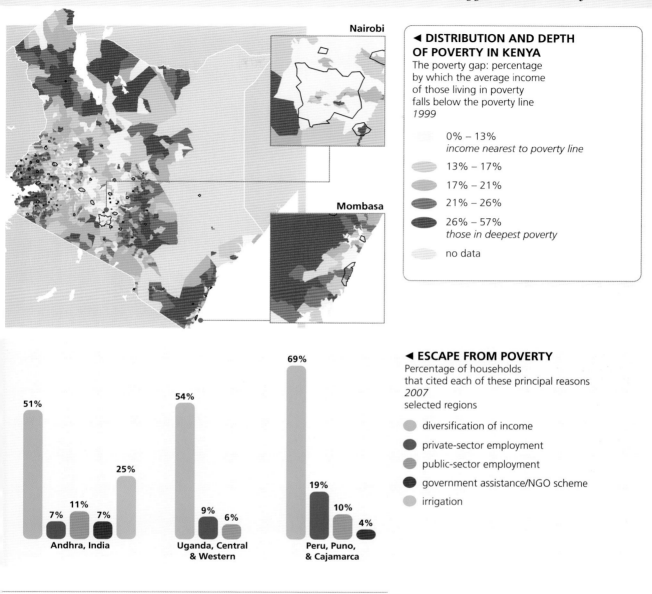

◄ DISTRIBUTION AND DEPTH OF POVERTY IN KENYA

The poverty gap: percentage by which the average income of those living in poverty falls below the poverty line
1999

- 0% – 13%
  income nearest to poverty line
- 13% – 17%
- 17% – 21%
- 21% – 26%
- 26% – 57%
  those in deepest poverty
- no data

Nairobi

Mombasa

◄ ESCAPE FROM POVERTY

Percentage of households that cited each of these principal reasons
2007
selected regions

- diversification of income
- private-sector employment
- public-sector employment
- government assistance/NGO scheme
- irrigation

Andhra, India: 51%, 7%, 11%, 7%, 25%

Uganda, Central & Western: 54%, 9%, 6%

Peru, Puno, & Cajamarca: 69%, 19%, 10%, 4%

consumption falls below a minimum acceptable level. The poverty gap measures how far, on average, income falls below that minimum level.

Research has tended to overlook additions to the ranks of the poor, but recent reconstruction of household trajectories in rural areas shows that illness, with its associated expenses and losses, constitutes the most frequent cause of descent into poverty. This new research also shows that diversification of livelihoods provides the common pathway for households to escape poverty. New forms of poverty mapping, such as the map of Kenya, analyze census data to identify the spatial concentration of different poverty measures. These broader understandings expand the range of possible actions to reduce poverty beyond questions of income, for example, to emphasize the kind of protection that may prevent the descent into poverty.

Almost
half
the global population lives on less than
$2.50
a day

Hunger

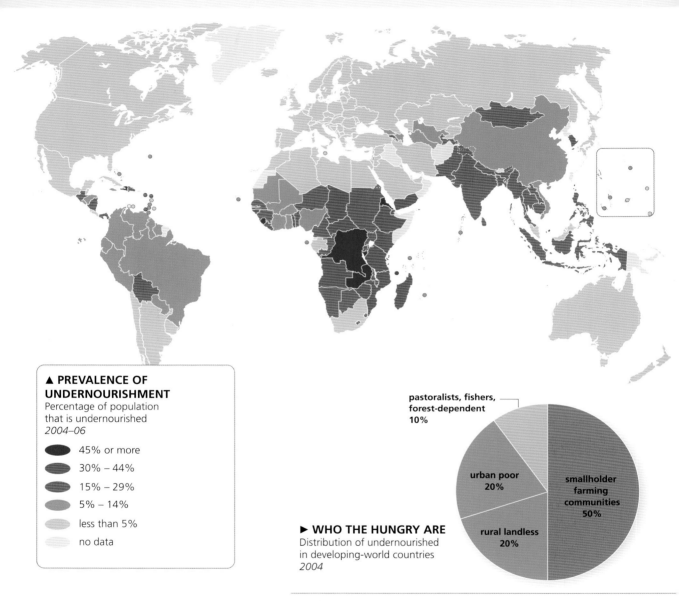

▲ PREVALENCE OF UNDERNOURISHMENT
Percentage of population that is undernourished
2004–06

- 45% or more
- 30% – 44%
- 15% – 29%
- 5% – 14%
- less than 5%
- no data

pastoralists, fishers, forest-dependent 10%

urban poor 20%

smallholder farming communities 50%

rural landless 20%

► WHO THE HUNGRY ARE
Distribution of undernourished in developing-world countries
2004

More than
1 billion people
do not have enough to eat – more than the combined populations of USA, Canada, and EU

► Differences in access to food constitute a devastating dimension of inequality. The UN World Food Programme argues that this is the number one risk to global health. Chronic hunger or under-nutrition can be defined as sustained nutritional deprivation. Although it receives less international attention than food crises that cause starvation, chronic under-nutrition affects many more people worldwide.

There are major disparities in food intake between developed and developing nations. The countries with the highest prevalence of under-nutrition are largely found in Sub-Saharan Africa. However, India contains the largest number of undernourished people.

Hunger is not the result of scarcity, but a lack of "command over food". Most people in the world obtain food by buying it. Some hundreds of

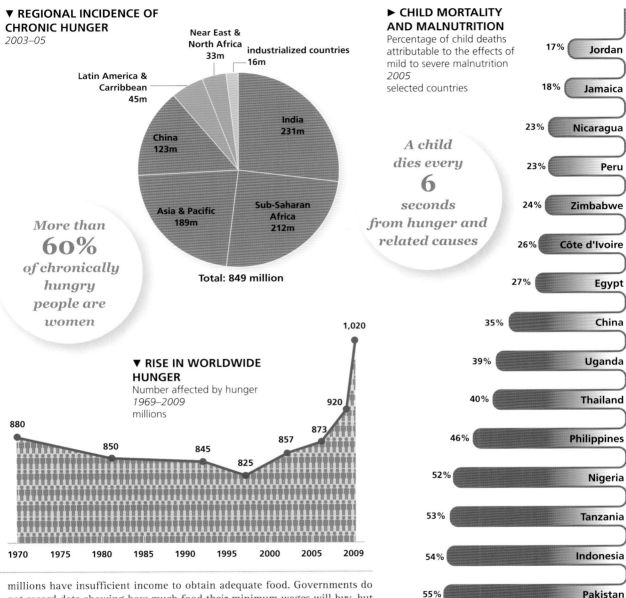

▼ REGIONAL INCIDENCE OF CHRONIC HUNGER
2003–05

Near East & North Africa
33m

industrialized countries
16m

Latin America & Carribbean
45m

India
231m

China
123m

Asia & Pacific
189m

Sub-Saharan Africa
212m

Total: 849 million

More than
60%
of chronically hungry people are women

► CHILD MORTALITY AND MALNUTRITION
Percentage of child deaths attributable to the effects of mild to severe malnutrition
2005
selected countries

A child dies every
6
seconds from hunger and related causes

17%	Jordan
18%	Jamaica
23%	Nicaragua
23%	Peru
24%	Zimbabwe
26%	Côte d'Ivoire
27%	Egypt
35%	China
39%	Uganda
40%	Thailand
46%	Philippines
52%	Nigeria
53%	Tanzania
54%	Indonesia
55%	Pakistan
65%	Nepal
66%	Bangladesh
67%	India

▼ RISE IN WORLDWIDE HUNGER
Number affected by hunger
1969–2009
millions

880 — 850 — 845 — 825 — 857 — 873 — 920 — 1,020

1970   1975   1980   1985   1990   1995   2000   2005   2009

millions have insufficient income to obtain adequate food. Governments do not record data showing how much food their minimum wages will buy, but in large parts of Africa and South Asia they are insufficient to sustain healthy life.

Children represent 25 percent of the world's hungry people. This presents a unique problem because proper nutrition is critical to physical and mental development. Mild and severe malnutrition in children are also underlying causes in death due to disease.

Poverty and under-nutrition are frequently linked, and when food prices rise, more people go hungry. Although the proportion of people who are hungry has generally been decreasing, the actual number of undernourished people has been rising.

Household Water

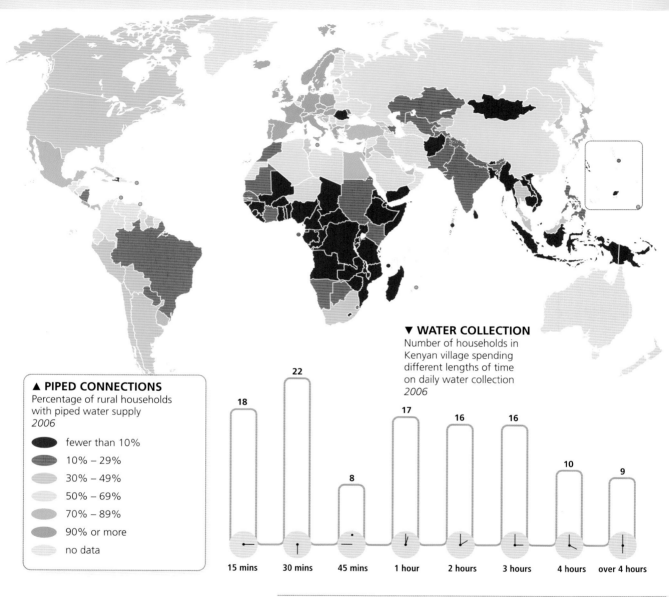

▲ PIPED CONNECTIONS

Percentage of rural households
with piped water supply
2006

- fewer than 10%
- 10% – 29%
- 30% – 49%
- 50% – 69%
- 70% – 89%
- 90% or more
- no data

▼ WATER COLLECTION
Number of households in
Kenyan village spending
different lengths of time
on daily water collection
2006

| 18 | 22 | 8 | 17 | 16 | 16 | 10 | 9 |
| 15 mins | 30 mins | 45 mins | 1 hour | 2 hours | 3 hours | 4 hours | over 4 hours |

Definition of improved source of water

- public tap or standpipe
- pipe water to dwelling, yard or plot
- protected spring
- protected dug well
- tube well or borehole
- rainwater collection

▶ Access to clean water is a key factor in development. People who obtain their household water from a safe, nearby source are likely not only to live longer, but to be better educated, and to have more life opportunities.

The wealth and social changes associated with industrialization allow governments and private utilities to provide piped domestic water to nearly all citizens. The provision of a clean water supply is considered responsible for two-thirds of the reduction in child mortality in early 20th-century US cities. In the early 21st century, however, there is still huge international inequality.

This is particularly marked in rural areas, where a piped domestic water supply is a rarity in most developing countries. The burden of collecting water, sometimes from long distances, falls mainly on women and children,

Poor people and those living in rural areas are least likely
to have easy access to safe drinking water.

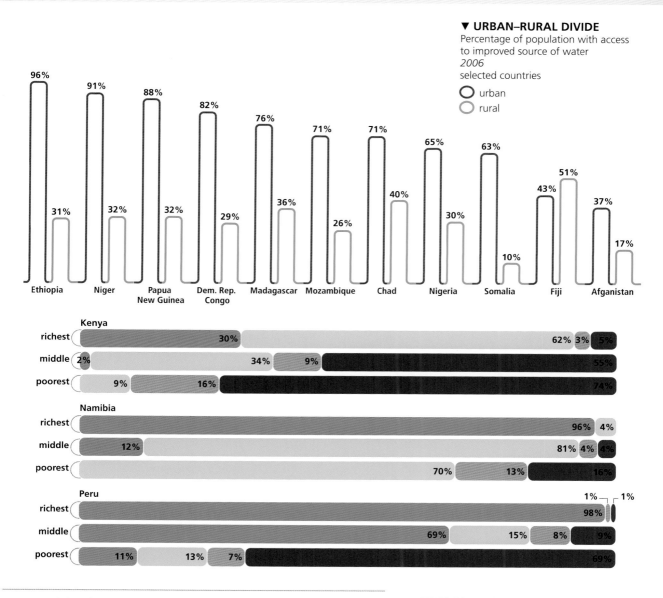

▼ URBAN–RURAL DIVIDE
Percentage of population with access
to improved source of water
2006
selected countries

○ urban
○ rural

Ethiopia: 96% / 31%
Niger: 91% / 32%
Papua New Guinea: 88% / 32%
Dem. Rep. Congo: 82% / 29%
Madagascar: 76% / 36%
Mozambique: 71% / 26%
Chad: 71% / 40%
Nigeria: 65% / 30%
Somalia: 63% / 10%
Fiji: 43% / 51%
Afganistan: 37% / 17%

Kenya
- richest: 30% | 62% | 3% | 5%
- middle: 2% | 34% | 9% | 55%
- poorest: 9% | 16% | 74%

Namibia
- richest: 96% | 4%
- middle: 12% | 81% | 4% | 4%
- poorest: 70% | 13% | 16%

Peru
- richest: 98% | 1% | 1%
- middle: 69% | 15% | 8% | 9%
- poorest: 11% | 13% | 7% | 69%

constraining the time they can spend on income generation, farming or
education. Global reports frequently cite the proportion of the population
with "improved" water access, meaning that water is obtained through a
technology such as a borehole, standpipe or protected well, which provide
relatively safe water. But such technologies do not necessarily reduce the
work of water collection. A dozen countries fail to provide even this
inadequate measure of access to half their population, with their rural
populations particularly badly served.

Within countries, the differences between the rich and poor are marked.
Even in poor countries, a large proportion of the wealthiest households
have a piped water supply.

▲ PIPES FOR RICH, PONDS FOR POOR
Percentage in different income groups
with access to a range of water supplies
2008 or latest available

richest = fifth of population on highest income
middle = fifth of population on middle income
poorest = fifth of population on lowest income

● piped water
○ improved source
◐ unimproved source
● surface water

Energy

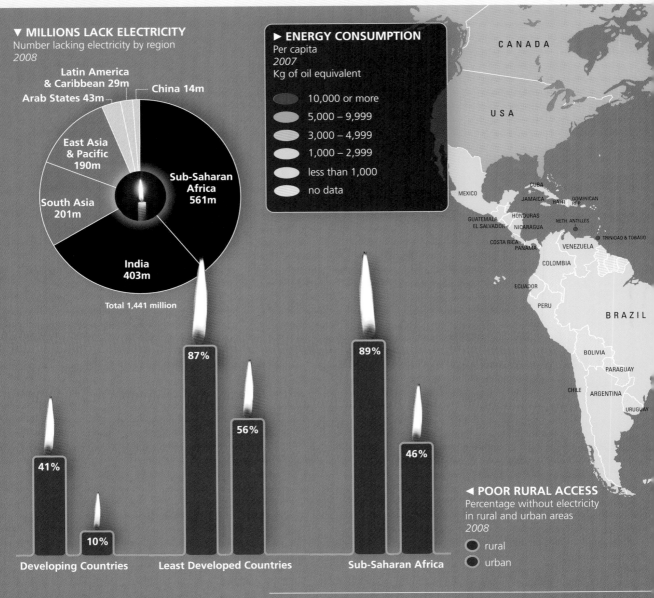

▼ MILLIONS LACK ELECTRICITY
Number lacking electricity by region
2008

- Latin America & Caribbean 29m
- Arab States 43m
- China 14m
- East Asia & Pacific 190m
- South Asia 201m
- Sub-Saharan Africa 561m
- India 403m

Total 1,441 million

▶ ENERGY CONSUMPTION
Per capita
2007
Kg of oil equivalent

- 10,000 or more
- 5,000 – 9,999
- 3,000 – 4,999
- 1,000 – 2,999
- less than 1,000
- no data

CANADA

USA

MEXICO
CUBA
JAMAICA
HAITI
DOMINICAN REP
NETH. ANTILLES
GUATEMALA
EL SALVADOR
HONDURAS
NICARAGUA
COSTA RICA
PANAMA
TRINIDAD & TOBAGO
VENEZUELA
COLOMBIA
ECUADOR
PERU
BRAZIL
BOLIVIA
PARAGUAY
CHILE
ARGENTINA
URUGUAY

Developing Countries
41%
10%

Least Developed Countries
87%
56%

Sub-Saharan Africa
89%
46%

◀ POOR RURAL ACCESS
Percentage without electricity
in rural and urban areas
2008

- ● rural
- ● urban

More than
80%
*of people
without electricity live in
Sub-Saharan Africa
or South Asia*

▶ Energy is central to fulfilling basic human needs, including the provision of access to clean water, heating, cooking, and healthcare, and to the advance of industry, agriculture and services. Yet, some 1.6 billion people in developing countries lack access to electricity, among them three-quarters of the population of Sub-Saharan Africa.

While urban dwellers may have sporadic access to power, electricity in rural areas is available for only a small minority. Energy can be used to pump irrigation water, thereby improving agricultural productivity, and it can boost a local economy, providing opportunities for training and jobs. Lack of energy discourages educated workers, such as teachers and doctors, from living and working in an area.

Energy is a prerequisite for economic opportunities and human development that remains inaccessible to many due to poverty, rural location, or lack of infrastructure.

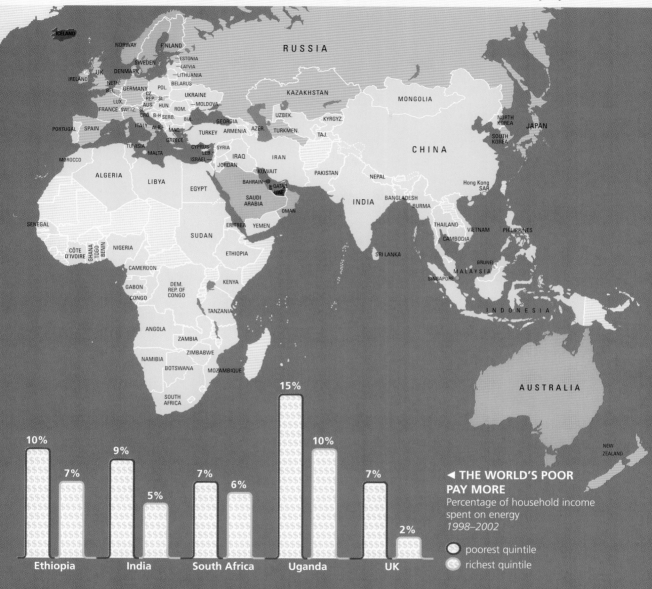

◄ THE WORLD'S POOR PAY MORE
Percentage of household income spent on energy
1998–2002

● poorest quintile
◐ richest quintile

Ethiopia 10% 7%
India 9% 5%
South Africa 7% 6%
Uganda 15% 10%
UK 7% 2%

Factories, agriculture, commerce, offices, and transport all require energy. Some economic models suggest there is a strong link between energy supply and economic growth, particularly at an intermediate stage of development. Energy was key to growth in Turkey, Korea, Brazil and Mexico, and there is evidence to suggest that a lack of available energy may have restricted growth in India.

Lack of energy infrastructure in many developing countries impedes the advance of human capabilities and freedoms. Most of those who lack access to electricity live in Sub-Saharan Africa and South Asia, particularly in rural areas. Few countries have tackled this inequality as well as China, which brought electricity to almost 700 million people between 1980 and 2000, achieving 98 percent access.

*The **18%** of people living in OECD countries are responsible for **45%** of the world's energy consumption*

Household Fuel

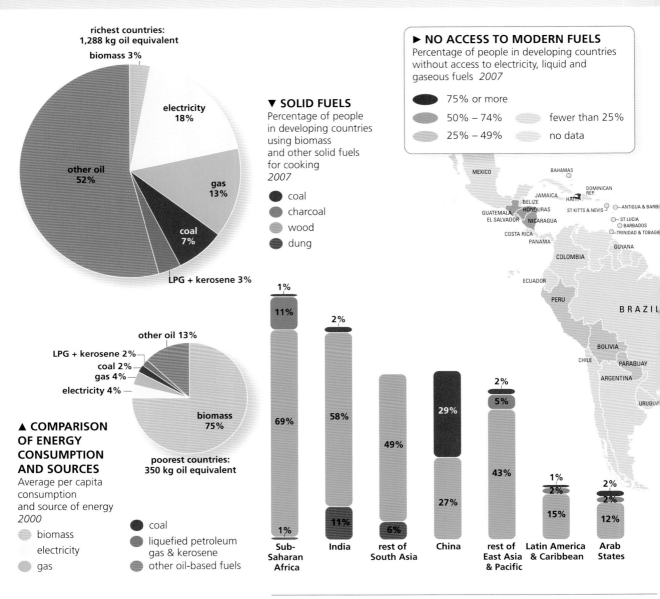

richest countries:
1,288 kg oil equivalent

- biomass 3%
- electricity 18%
- other oil 52%
- gas 13%
- coal 7%
- LPG + kerosene 3%

▼ SOLID FUELS
Percentage of people in developing countries using biomass and other solid fuels for cooking *2007*

- coal
- charcoal
- wood
- dung

► NO ACCESS TO MODERN FUELS
Percentage of people in developing countries without access to electricity, liquid and gaseous fuels *2007*

- 75% or more
- 50% – 74%
- 25% – 49%
- fewer than 25%
- no data

▲ COMPARISON OF ENERGY CONSUMPTION AND SOURCES
Average per capita consumption and source of energy *2000*

- biomass
- electricity
- gas
- coal
- liquefied petroleum gas & kerosene
- other oil-based fuels

poorest countries:
350 kg oil equivalent

- other oil 13%
- LPG + kerosene 2%
- coal 2%
- gas 4%
- electricity 4%
- biomass 75%

Solid fuels bar chart

Sub-Saharan Africa	1%, 11%, 69%, 1%
India	2%, 58%, 11%
rest of South Asia	49%, 6%
China	29%, 27%
rest of East Asia & Pacific	2%, 5%, 43%
Latin America & Caribbean	1%, 2%, 15%
Arab States	2%, 2%, 12%

Map labels: MEXICO, BAHAMAS, DOMINICAN REP., JAMAICA, HAITI, BELIZE, HONDURAS, ST KITTS & NEVIS, ANTIGUA & BARBI, GUATEMALA, EL SALVADOR, NICARAGUA, ST LUCIA, BARBADOS, COSTA RICA, PANAMA, TRINIDAD & TOBAG, GUYANA, COLOMBIA, ECUADOR, PERU, BRAZIL, BOLIVIA, CHILE, PARAGUAY, ARGENTINA, URUGUA

Over **75%** *of global energy used is from modern fuels, yet in developing countries more than half of people do not have access to them*

► More than half of people in developing countries rely primarily on cheap, yet hazardous, solid fuel and biomass – coal, charcoal, wood, dung, and crop residues – for their cooking needs and limited indoor heating and lighting. By comparison, virtually everyone in the industrialized world has access to the more efficient and flexible "modern" fuels – electricity, oil and gas. These fuels can support a variety of household uses, including refrigeration and other appliances, transportation, and access to telecommunications and technology.

Dependence on wood as household fuel requires people – usually women and children – to travel long distances, sometimes to the receding edges of forests, to gather branches and carry them home.

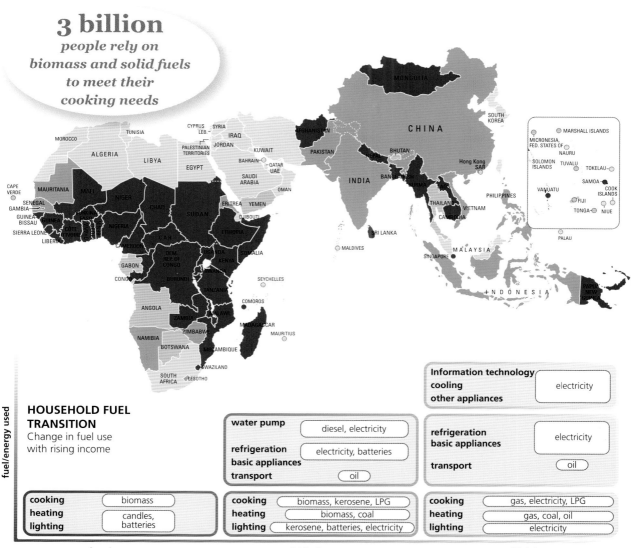

3 billion
*people rely on
biomass and solid fuels
to meet their
cooking needs*

HOUSEHOLD FUEL TRANSITION

Change in fuel use
with rising income

fuel/energy used

| | Information technology cooling other appliances | electricity |

	water pump	diesel, electricity
	refrigeration basic appliances	electricity, batteries
	transport	oil

| | refrigeration basic appliances | electricity |
| | transport | oil |

| **cooking** | biomass |
| **heating** lighting | candles, batteries |

cooking	biomass, kerosene, LPG
heating	biomass, coal
lighting	kerosene, batteries, electricity

cooking	gas, electricity, LPG
heating	gas, coal, oil
lighting	electricity

low income   **middle income**   **high income**

Biomass fuels tend to be used in open fires or inefficient stoves. Improved cooking stoves, which use less fuel and produce less indoor pollution, are not widely used. More flexible and cost-effective energy technologies are needed to improve living conditions. Ideally, these should involve renewable energies to avoid increasing greenhouse gas emissions.

Biomass fuels, when used on an open fire or inefficient stove, produce a lot of smoke inside dwellings, which can lead to lung cancer, child pneumonia, and chronic obstructive pulmonary disease. These undesirable household fuels form the bottom rung of the energy ladder. As people make the transition from low-income to higher-income groups, they are able to adopt modern fuels to generate energy for a wider range of uses.

More than
70%
*of people in developing
countries
who cook with solid fuels
have no access to
improved stoves*

Mobility

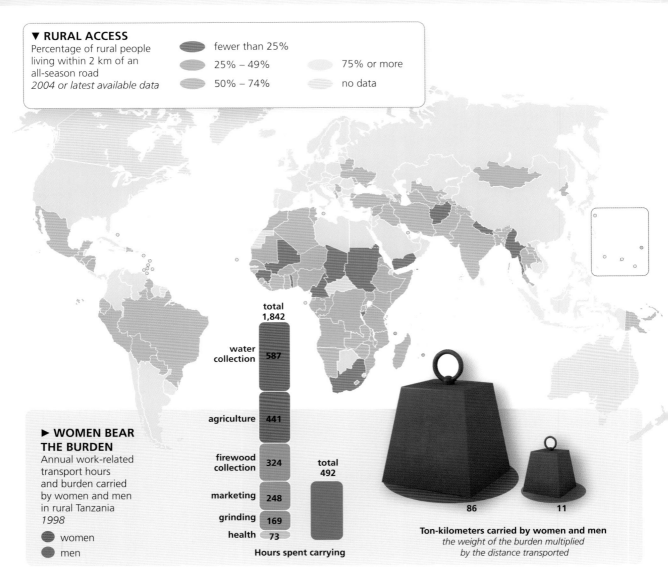

▼ RURAL ACCESS
Percentage of rural people living within 2 km of an all-season road
2004 or latest available data

- fewer than 25%
- 25% – 49%
- 50% – 74%
- 75% or more
- no data

▶ WOMEN BEAR THE BURDEN
Annual work-related transport hours and burden carried by women and men in rural Tanzania
1998

- women
- men

total 1,842

water collection	587
agriculture	441
firewood collection	324
marketing	248
grinding	169
health	73

total 492

Hours spent carrying

86   11

Ton-kilometers carried by women and men
the weight of the burden multiplied by the distance transported

People in high-income countries are **over 30 times more mobile** *than those in low-income countries*

▶ Access to travel opens opportunities, but methods of travel and distances covered are influenced by industrialization and social class. People in industrialized countries, wealthy people in developing countries, and those in urban environments, are generally more mobile than the less well-off.

Many inhabitants of rural Africa, Latin America and Asia live further than 2 kilometers (up to 25 minutes walk) from an all-season road, constraining their opportunities to work away from home, visit a health clinic, and take their produce to market.

The diversity of modes of travel in developing countries, including the use of rickshaws, cycle rickshaws, hand carts, scooter taxis, motorcycles and mini-bus taxis, indicates widespread innovation in the use of human and motor power. This may increase transport opportunities, but sometimes,

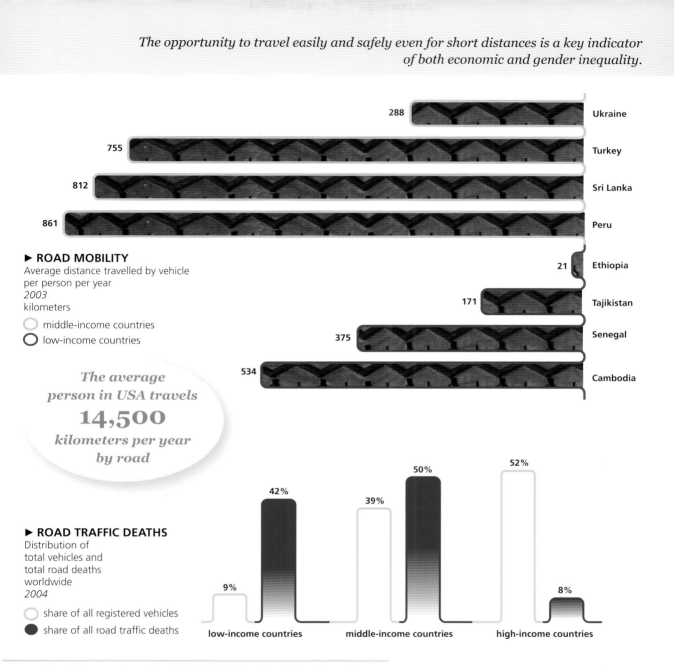

288 Ukraine

755 Turkey

812 Sri Lanka

861 Peru

21 Ethiopia

171 Tajikistan

375 Senegal

534 Cambodia

▶ ROAD MOBILITY
Average distance travelled by vehicle
per person per year
2003
kilometers

○ middle-income countries
⬤ low-income countries

*The average
person in USA travels*
14,500
*kilometers per year
by road*

▶ ROAD TRAFFIC DEATHS
Distribution of
total vehicles and
total road deaths
worldwide
2004

○ share of all registered vehicles
⬤ share of all road traffic deaths

9% 42% — low-income countries
39% 50% — middle-income countries
52% 8% — high-income countries

as with rickshaws, at considerable health risk to those doing the work.

Even when people in lower- and middle-income countries do have the opportunity to travel, their path to work, school or markets is frequently more dangerous than a similar journey in a high-income country. Unsafe modes of transport, in conjunction with insufficient highway regulation, are major causes of road accidents and deaths. Although only 48 percent of the world's registered vehicles are found in low- and middle-income countries, that is where 91 percent of road fatalities occur.

In addition to differences between rich and poor, there are often stark inequalities between women and men. For example, women in rural Africa tend to carry much heavier burdens, over greater distances, than men do.

1 billion
*rural people live
further than 2 kilometers
from an all-season road*

Digital Divide

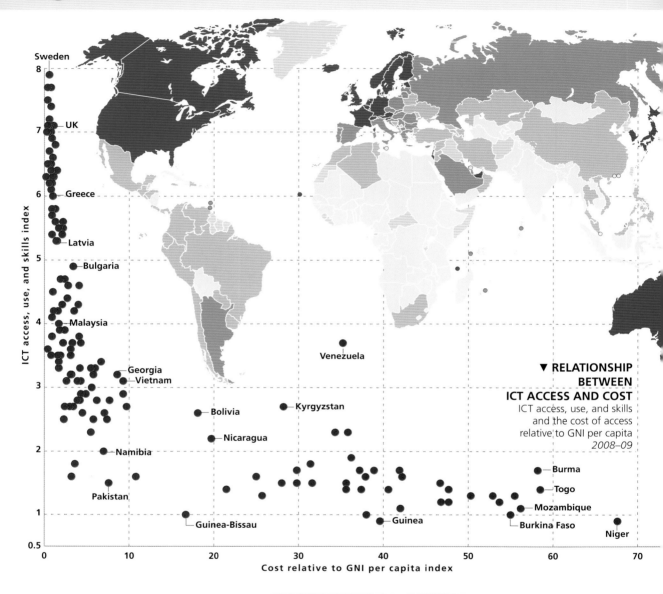

▼ RELATIONSHIP BETWEEN ICT ACCESS AND COST
ICT access, use, and skills and the cost of access relative to GNI per capita
2008–09

Axis labels:
ICT access, use, and skills index

Cost relative to GNI per capita index

Data point labels (as plotted): Sweden, UK, Greece, Latvia, Bulgaria, Malaysia, Georgia, Vietnam, Venezuela, Bolivia, Kyrgyzstan, Nicaragua, Namibia, Pakistan, Guinea-Bissau, Guinea, Burma, Togo, Mozambique, Burkina Faso, Niger

2009 cell phone use:
developing countries
57%
industrialized countries
100%

▶ Information and communications technologies (ICTs) support economic growth, provide new avenues for livelihoods, and expand capabilities to meet basic needs and freedoms. Thus, cell phones and the internet provide increased access to knowledge on a wide range of issues, including healthcare, nutrition, education, crop yields, and market prices. People in remote and poorly serviced areas can seek medical advice, extend their education, and conduct business, leading to healthier, better-qualified citizens, with more productive livelihoods.

The use of cell phones is growing rapidly in developing countries (extending to more than 50 percent of the population in 2009), but internet access remains low. In Africa, in 2009, only 9 percent of the population had

The digital divide between industrialized and non-industrialized countries constrains the advance of healthcare, education, social freedoms, and livelihoods.

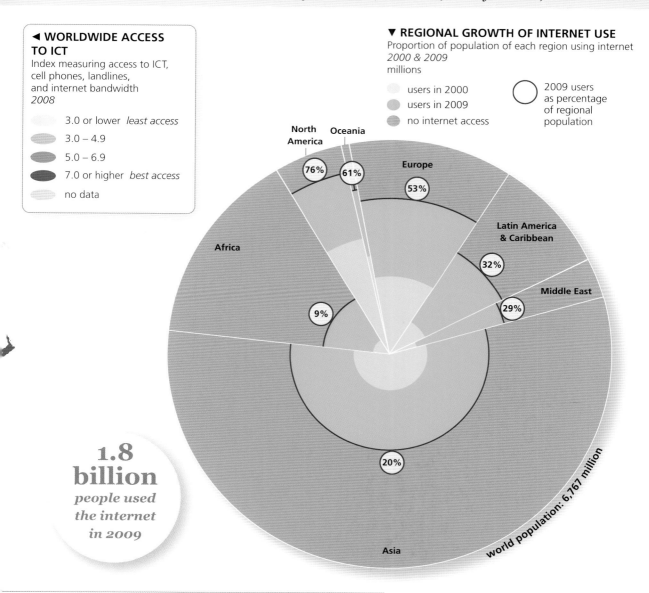

◄ WORLDWIDE ACCESS TO ICT

Index measuring access to ICT, cell phones, landlines, and internet bandwidth
2008

- 3.0 or lower *least access*
- 3.0 – 4.9
- 5.0 – 6.9
- 7.0 or higher *best access*
- no data

▼ REGIONAL GROWTH OF INTERNET USE

Proportion of population of each region using internet
2000 & 2009
millions

- users in 2000
- users in 2009
- no internet access

2009 users as percentage of regional population

North America 76%

Oceania 61%

Europe 53%

Latin America & Caribbean 32%

Middle East 29%

Africa 9%

Asia 20%

world population: 6,767 million

1.8 billion
people used the internet in 2009

internet access, and in Asia 20 percent. In comparison, 53 percent of Europeans had access, and 76 percent of North Americans. The gap in access to high-speed broadband is even worse, due to price and lack of infrastructure in developing regions.

The digital divide exists between the educated and the non-educated, between the young and the elderly, between the urban and the rural population, and, to a lesser extent (and with the gap closing fast), between males and females.

Maximizing the benefits of ICT depends not only on access, but also on the growth of skills and the breadth of applications to facilitate an inclusive information society that accelerates human development.

Only 1 in 5 people in developing countries has access to the internet

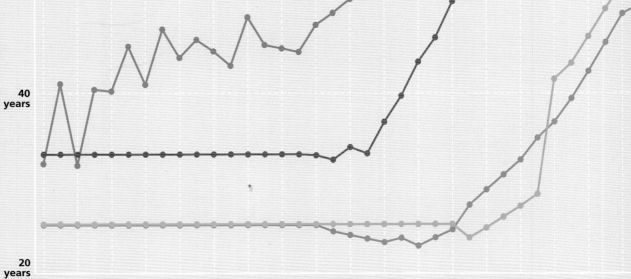

▼ **INCREASED LIFE EXPECTANCY**
At birth
1800–2009

— Sweden
— Argentina
— India
— Kenya

90 years

80 years

60 years

40 years

20 years

1800 1810 1820 1830 1840 1850 1860 1870 1880 1890 1900 1910 1920 1930 1940 1950 1960 1970

Health Inequalities 5

► Health inequalities between countries have decreased throughout the past century, as human health and life expectancy have generally improved. This is largely due to better public health and sanitation, increased access to medicine and health technology, and higher standards of living and education.

The proportion of underweight children worldwide declined from 25 percent in 1990 to 18 percent in 2005. The prevalence of TB is falling, and most countries appear to be on course to meet the Millennium Development Goal for reducing the malaria burden. HIV, which has devastated the adult populations of much of southern Africa, appears to be coming under control, with the rate of new infections declining by 16 percent between 2000 and 2008.

Despite improvements in health, there are significant inequalities between the developed and the industrialized worlds, and between rich and poor, urban and the rural within most countries. Socioeconomic factors such as level of education – in particular that of the mother – occupation, and ethnicity are also major contributors to health inequities. Maternal mortality is the health indicator that shows the widest gap, varying from 27 deaths per 100,000 live births in the European region to 900 in Africa. The global rate has also remained stagnant at 400 deaths per 100,000 live births between 1990 and 2005.

Communicable diseases such as HIV/AIDS, tuberculosis, and malaria are treatable and preventable, but account for over two-thirds of the years of life lost (YLL) in low-income countries. By contrast, in middle-income countries, these account for less than 25 percent of YLL, and under 10 percent in high-income countries, where the major causes of death are the non-communicable cardiovascular diseases, cancer, Alzheimer's, and diabetes.

The key health risk factors in low-income countries are unsafe water, lack of sanitation, use of solid fuels in households, childhood under-nutrition, and poor infant feeding practices; and in high-income countries, the risk factors are obesity, harmful consumption of alcohol, and tobacco.

Cross-national comparisons have shown that governments can make changes and implement programs to reduce inequalities. Low-cost primary healthcare and health education have reduced inequalities for the poor in Sri Lanka, Cuba, and Costa Rica, resulting in higher life expectancy and reduced illness compared with other countries at similar income levels.

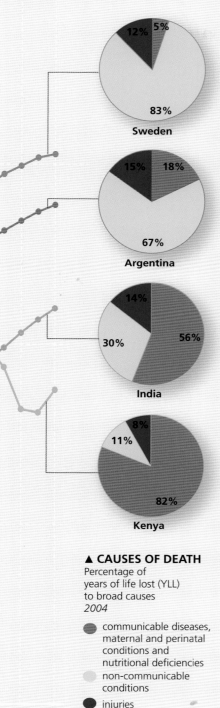

Sweden — 5%, 12%, 83%

Argentina — 18%, 15%, 67%

India — 14%, 30%, 56%

Kenya — 8%, 11%, 82%

▲ **CAUSES OF DEATH**
Percentage of years of life lost (YLL) to broad causes
2004

- communicable diseases, maternal and perinatal conditions and nutritional deficiencies
- non-communicable conditions
- injuries

80   1990   2000   2009

67

Life Expectancy

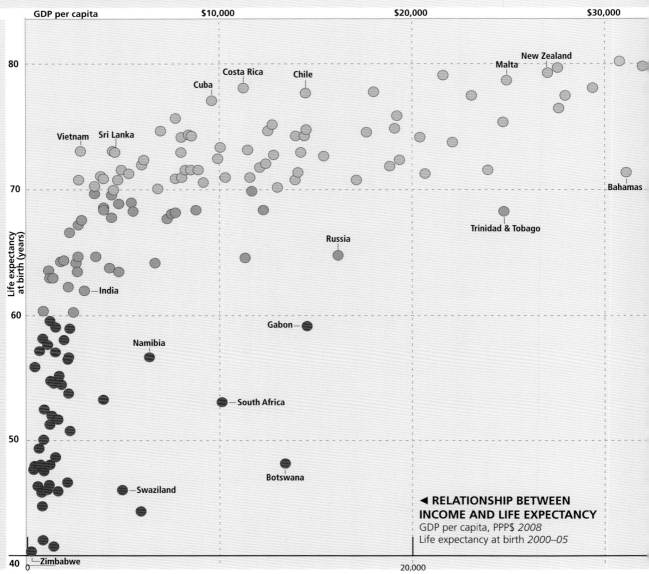

◄ **RELATIONSHIP BETWEEN
INCOME AND LIFE EXPECTANCY**
GDP per capita, PPP$ *2008*
Life expectancy at birth *2000–05*

*A child born in
central Africa is
likely to live only*
half as long
*as one born in
western Europe*

▶ Life expectancy at birth is a measure of the number of years a newborn is expected to live if current mortality rates continue to apply. It provides a robust measure of the health of a country's population, and also of the level of inequality within it.

Until the 1990s, life expectancy was steadily rising in almost all parts of the world. Then HIV/AIDS became a major cause of death in Sub-Saharan Africa, and the disruptions of economic transition in Eastern Europe brought life expectancy decline there, too. In some countries of southern Africa, such as Botswana, life expectancy declined by 10 years or more during the 1990s as a result of AIDS deaths. In Russia it declined from 69 to 64 in the five years after 1989.

Longer life expectancy is associated with increased national income,

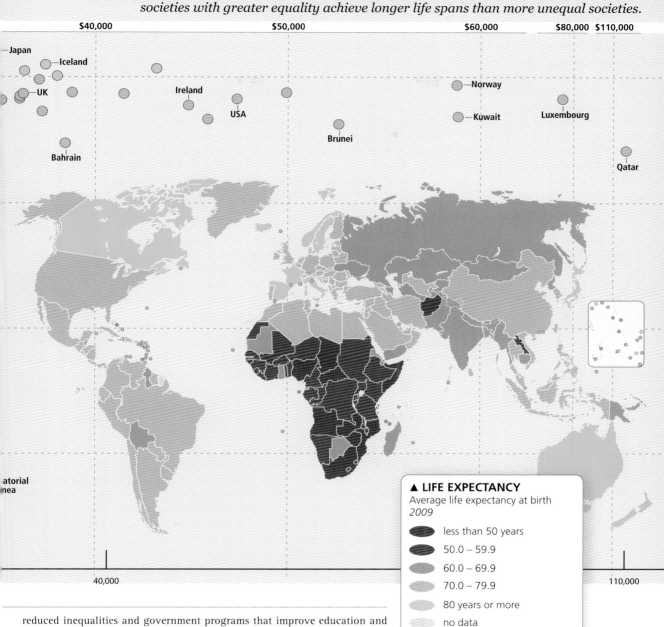

Societies with higher GDP tend to have higher life expectancy. At all levels of GDP, however, societies with greater equality achieve longer life spans than more unequal societies.

$40,000 $50,000 $60,000 $80,000 $110,000

Japan
Iceland
UK
Ireland
USA
Brunei
Bahrain
Norway
Kuwait
Luxembourg
Qatar

Equatorial Guinea

40,000   110,000

▲ **LIFE EXPECTANCY**
Average life expectancy at birth
2009

- less than 50 years
- 50.0 – 59.9
- 60.0 – 69.9
- 70.0 – 79.9
- 80 years or more
- no data

reduced inequalities and government programs that improve education and health, in particular for the poor. That is why people in Sri Lanka, Cuba and Costa Rica have high life expectancy compared with other countries of a similar income level. By contrast, people in South Africa and Brazil have lower average life expectancy than other societies of a similar income level because their histories are characterized by marked inequality and neglect of the needs of the poor.

The influence of social and economic change on life expectancy is also illustrated by the example of the industrializing countries of Europe from the 18th to 20th centuries, where dramatic increases in life expectancy pre-dated advances in curative medicine such as antibiotics.

Life expectancy in Africa:
54 years
in North America:
79 years

Maternal Mortality

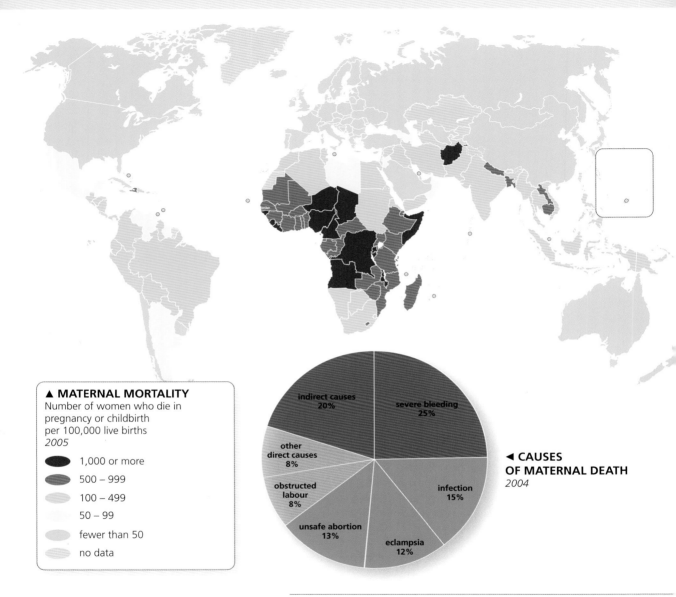

▲ MATERNAL MORTALITY
Number of women who die in
pregnancy or childbirth
per 100,000 live births
2005

- 1,000 or more
- 500 – 999
- 100 – 499
- 50 – 99
- fewer than 50
- no data

**◄ CAUSES
OF MATERNAL DEATH**
2004

Pie chart: severe bleeding 25%, infection 15%, eclampsia 12%, unsafe abortion 13%, obstructed labour 8%, other direct causes 8%, indirect causes 20%

There are
534,000
*maternal deaths
each year.*
50% *are in
Sub-Saharan Africa;*
45% *in Asia.*

► Maternal mortality – the death of a woman during or immediately after pregnancy – is one of the wider global inequalities. There is a greater disparity between rich and poor nations in maternal mortality rates than in any other commonly used public health indicator. This is because maternal mortality rates cannot be easily improved through targeted interventions. Improvements to the whole health system are required: greater administrative, technical, and logistical capacity, sustained financial investment, and an increased number of skilled health personnel.

Each pregnancy in a developing country is, on average, 50 times more likely to lead to a woman's death than a pregnancy in an industrialized country. Most of the direct causes of maternal deaths – hemorrhage, obstructed labor, unsafe abortion, sepsis/infections, and pregnancy-related

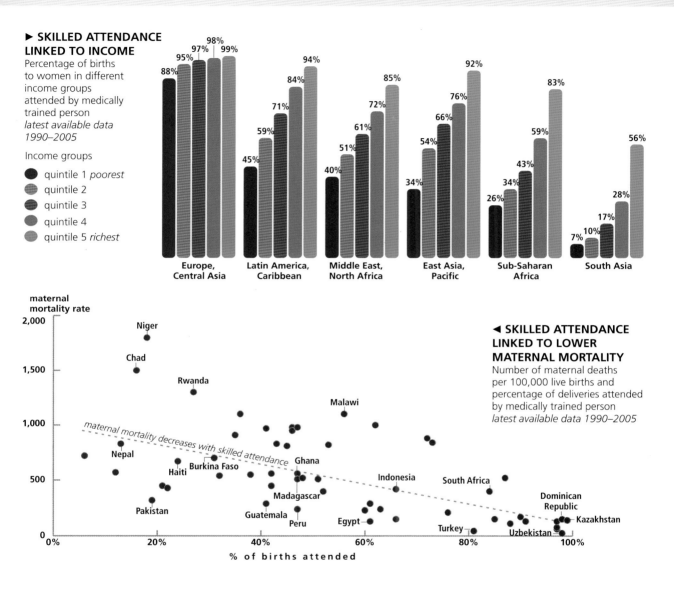

▶ **SKILLED ATTENDANCE LINKED TO INCOME**

Percentage of births to women in different income groups attended by medically trained person
latest available data 1990–2005

Income groups

- quintile 1 *poorest*
- quintile 2
- quintile 3
- quintile 4
- quintile 5 *richest*

Europe, Central Asia: 88% 95% 97% 98% 99%
Latin America, Caribbean: 45% 59% 71% 84% 94%
Middle East, North Africa: 40% 51% 61% 72% 85%
East Asia, Pacific: 34% 54% 66% 76% 92%
Sub-Saharan Africa: 26% 34% 43% 59% 83%
South Asia: 7% 10% 17% 28% 56%

maternal mortality rate

◀ **SKILLED ATTENDANCE LINKED TO LOWER MATERNAL MORTALITY**

Number of maternal deaths per 100,000 live births and percentage of deliveries attended by medically trained person
latest available data 1990–2005

maternal mortality decreases with skilled attendance

Niger, Chad, Rwanda, Malawi, Nepal, Haiti, Burkina Faso, Ghana, Indonesia, South Africa, Pakistan, Madagascar, Guatemala, Peru, Egypt, Turkey, Dominican Republic, Kazakhstan, Uzbekistan

% of births attended

hypertensive disorders (eclampsia) – are preventable with proper prenatal and antenatal care. Countries with higher proportions of deliveries with a skilled attendant present have lower maternal mortality rates.

There are wide variations within countries. Impoverished and rural women are far less likely than urban or wealthier women to receive skilled care during childbirth. Women in the wealthiest quintile are six times more likely to deliver their baby with a health professional in attendance than those in the poorest quintile. In Chad, only 1 percent of the poorest women are attended, compared with 48 percent of the wealthiest women.

Many maternal deaths are attributable to indirect causes: illnesses aggravated by pregnancy, including anemia, malaria, HIV/AIDS, diseases of the heart, lung, liver, or kidneys.

A woman's chance of dying from pregnancy or childbirth:
Sub-Saharan Africa:
1 in 16
OECD countries:
1 in 3,800

Child Mortality

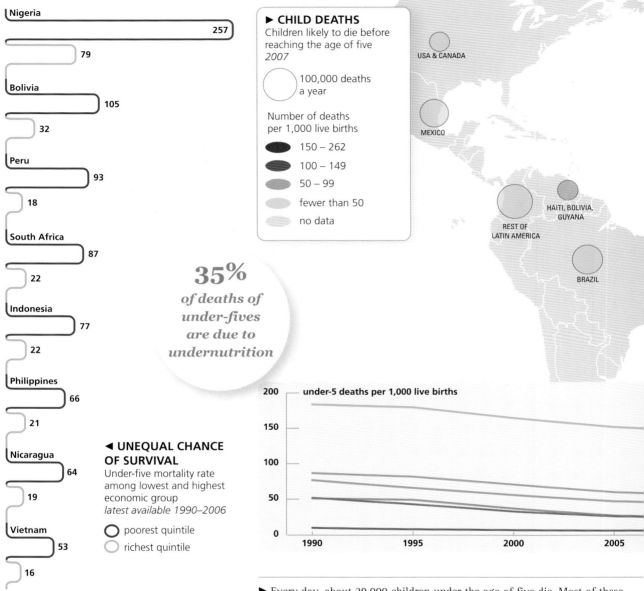

CHILD DEATHS
Children likely to die before reaching the age of five
2007

100,000 deaths a year

Number of deaths per 1,000 live births

- 150 – 262
- 100 – 149
- 50 – 99
- fewer than 50
- no data

USA & CANADA

MEXICO

REST OF LATIN AMERICA

HAITI, BOLIVIA, GUYANA

BRAZIL

Nigeria — 257
79
Bolivia — 105
32
Peru — 93
18
South Africa — 87
22
Indonesia — 77
22
Philippines — 66
21
Nicaragua — 64
19
Vietnam — 53
16

35%
of deaths of under-fives are due to undernutrition

◄ UNEQUAL CHANCE OF SURVIVAL
Under-five mortality rate among lowest and highest economic group
latest available 1990–2006

○ poorest quintile
○ richest quintile

under-5 deaths per 1,000 live births

200
150
100
50
0

1990   1995   2000   2005

Around
17 children die every minute
from largely preventable causes

► Every day, about 29,000 children under the age of five die. Most of these children are in developing countries and die from preventable causes. Half are in Sub-Saharan Africa and 42 percent in Asia.

There are large discrepancies in child mortality between the rich and the poor within a country. In many developing countries, under-five mortality is more than twice as high for the poorest fifth of the population, as for the wealthiest fifth, and in Nigeria it is over three times as high. Studies have shown that urban poor children have higher mortality than even their rural counterparts, due to lack of access to clean water and full vaccinations.

Since 1990, the global child mortality rate has declined by 28 percent, from 90 deaths per 1,000 live births to 65 in 2008. Despite this global

Children in developing countries become sick and often die of preventable or treatable diseases. Undernutrition, and lack of safe water and sanitation contribute to half of all child deaths.

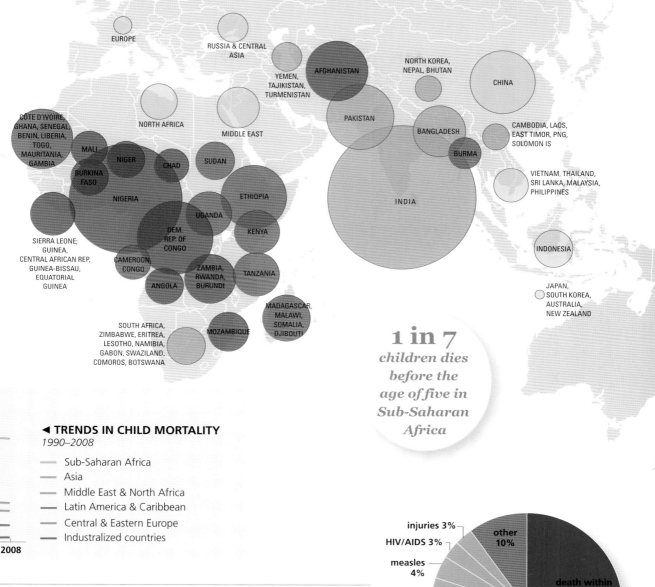

EUROPE

RUSSIA & CENTRAL ASIA

YEMEN, TAJIKISTAN, TURMENISTAN

AFGHANISTAN

NORTH KOREA, NEPAL, BHUTAN

CHINA

NORTH AFRICA

MIDDLE EAST

PAKISTAN

BANGLADESH

CAMBODIA, LAOS, EAST TIMOR, PNG, SOLOMON IS

BURMA

CÔTE D'IVOIRE, GHANA, SENEGAL, BENIN, LIBERIA, TOGO, MAURITANIA, GAMBIA

MALI

NIGER

CHAD

SUDAN

VIETNAM, THAILAND, SRI LANKA, MALAYSIA, PHILIPPINES

BURKINA FASO

NIGERIA

ETHIOPIA

UGANDA

INDIA

SIERRA LEONE; GUINEA, CENTRAL AFRICAN REP, GUINEA-BISSAU, EQUATORIAL GUINEA

DEM. REP. OF CONGO

KENYA

INDONESIA

CAMEROON, CONGO

ZAMBIA, RWANDA, BURUNDI

TANZANIA

ANGOLA

JAPAN, SOUTH KOREA, AUSTRALIA, NEW ZEALAND

SOUTH AFRICA, ZIMBABWE, ERITREA, LESOTHO, NAMIBIA, GABON, SWAZILAND, COMOROS, BOTSWANA

MOZAMBIQUE

MADAGASCAR, MALAWI, SOMALIA, DJIBOUTI

1 in 7
children dies before the age of five in Sub-Saharan Africa

◀ **TRENDS IN CHILD MORTALITY**
1990–2008

— Sub-Saharan Africa
— Asia
— Middle East & North Africa
— Latin America & Caribbean
— Central & Eastern Europe
— Industrialized countries

2008

progress, very high rates of child mortality continue to occur in Sub-Saharan Africa, with several countries experiencing a rise in rates from 1990 to 2007.

Most child deaths are attributable to preventable or treatable causes: pneumonia, diarrhea, malaria, preterm delivery, or lack of oxygen at birth. These deaths could be prevented by low-tech, cost-effective measures such as vaccines, antibiotics, oral rehydration therapy to combat dehydration from diarrhea, anti-malarial treatment, micronutrient supplementation, insecticide-treated bed nets, improved breastfeeding practices, increased access to primary healthcare services for women and their families, and improved drinking water and sanitation facilities in communities.

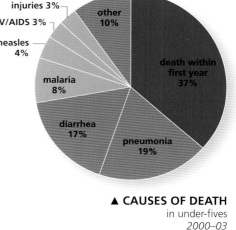

injuries 3%
HIV/AIDS 3%
measles 4%
malaria 8%
diarrhea 17%
pneumonia 19%
death within first year 37%
other 10%

▲ **CAUSES OF DEATH**
in under-fives
2000–03

74–75 Access to Healthcare; 84–85 Early Childhood Care & Education ▶

Access to Healthcare

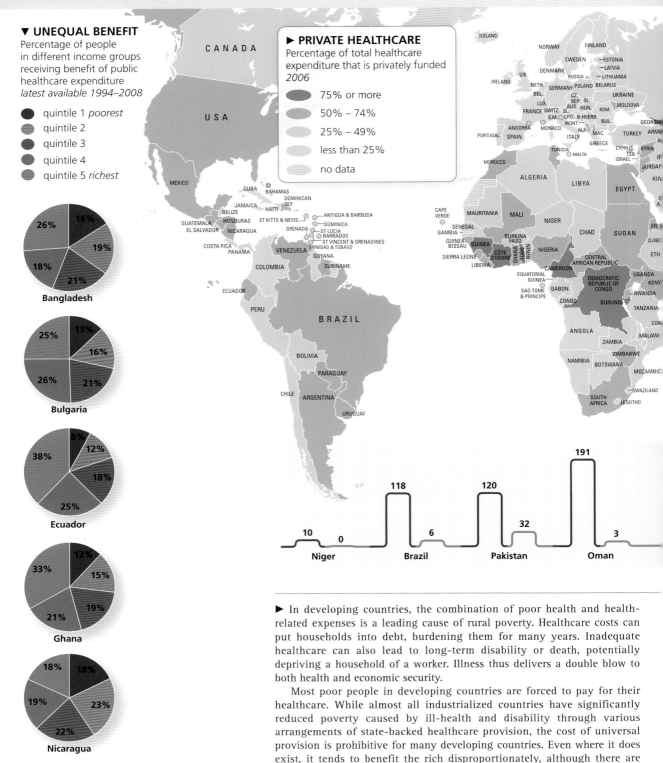

▼ UNEQUAL BENEFIT

Percentage of people in different income groups receiving benefit of public healthcare expenditure
latest available 1994–2008

- quintile 1 *poorest*
- quintile 2
- quintile 3
- quintile 4
- quintile 5 *richest*

Bangladesh
16%
19%
21%
18%
26%

Bulgaria
13%
16%
21%
26%
25%

Ecuador
8%
12%
18%
25%
38%

Ghana
12%
15%
19%
21%
33%

Nicaragua
18%
23%
22%
19%
18%

► PRIVATE HEALTHCARE

Percentage of total healthcare expenditure that is privately funded
2006

- 75% or more
- 50% – 74%
- 25% – 49%
- less than 25%
- no data

Niger 10 — 0
Brazil 118 — 6
Pakistan 120 — 32
Oman 191 — 3

► In developing countries, the combination of poor health and health-related expenses is a leading cause of rural poverty. Healthcare costs can put households into debt, burdening them for many years. Inadequate healthcare can also lead to long-term disability or death, potentially depriving a household of a worker. Illness thus delivers a double blow to both health and economic security.

Most poor people in developing countries are forced to pay for their healthcare. While almost all industrialized countries have significantly reduced poverty caused by ill-health and disability through various arrangements of state-backed healthcare provision, the cost of universal provision is prohibitive for many developing countries. Even where it does exist, it tends to benefit the rich disproportionately, although there are

Access to healthcare is worst in low-income countries, in rural areas and for the poor. The primary beneficiaries of government health expenditure, even when it is targeted at the poor, are the rich.

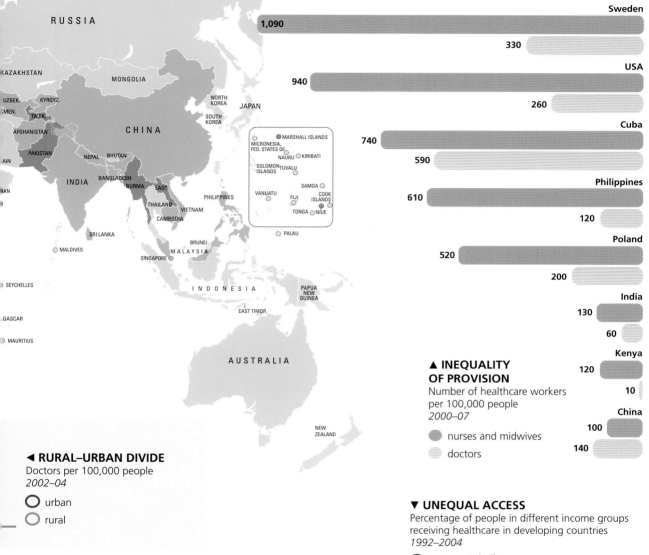

▲ INEQUALITY OF PROVISION

Number of healthcare workers per 100,000 people
2000–07

- nurses and midwives
- doctors

Sweden
1,090
330

USA
940
260

Cuba
740
590

Philippines
610
120

Poland
520
200

India
130
60

Kenya
120
10

China
100
140

◀ RURAL–URBAN DIVIDE

Doctors per 100,000 people
2002–04

- ⭕ urban
- ⭕ rural

▼ UNEQUAL ACCESS

Percentage of people in different income groups receiving healthcare in developing countries
1992–2004

- ● poorest quintile
- ● richest quintile

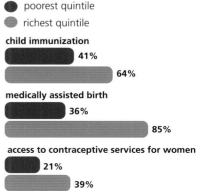

child immunization
41%
64%

medically assisted birth
36%
85%

access to contraceptive services for women
21%
39%

exceptions, including some countries that have adopted more socialized healthcare systems.

Both historical experience in industrialized countries and outstanding examples in the developing world, such as China and Cuba, show that low-cost primary healthcare provision can raise life expectancy and reduce illness. Nurses and community healthcare workers with limited training can provide many basic healthcare needs. In most developing countries, however, the provision of doctors and hospitals able to meet more complex health needs and emergencies is limited, particularly in rural areas. This lack has the greatest impact on the healthcare needs of the poor, and especially on those of poor women and children.

Infectious Diseases

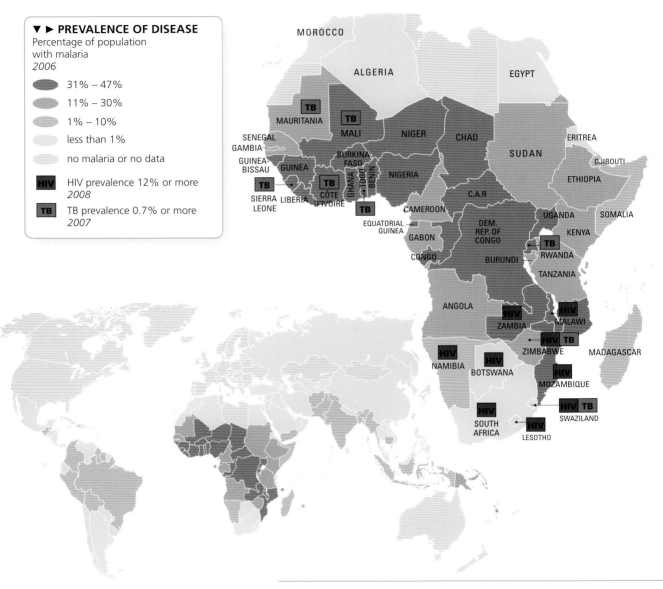

▼ ► PREVALENCE OF DISEASE
Percentage of population
with malaria
2006

- 31% – 47%
- 11% – 30%
- 1% – 10%
- less than 1%
- no malaria or no data

HIV HIV prevalence 12% or more
2008

TB TB prevalence 0.7% or more
2007

*Treatment of malaria
may account for up to*

40%

*of public health expenditure
in countries with a
heavy malaria burden*

► Every year in tropical regions, 247 million people become ill with malaria and over 1 million people die. Countries with high rates of malaria are often also those with high rates of poverty and low national incomes.

Globally, AIDS is the fourth most common cause of death. Its impact is most severe in Sub-Saharan Africa, but pandemics are also burgeoning in India, China and Russia, where the disease is predicted to significantly reduce future economic growth. HIV/AIDS intensifies the effects of poverty, which in turn contributes to the spread of infection. HIV/AIDS is increasingly becoming a disease with a face that is young, African and female, with the infection rate among women now higher than that among men, due to biological and socio-economic factors.

Malaria, HIV/AIDS, and tuberculosis are having a devastating impact on the poorest and most vulnerable people in developing countries, notably in Africa and South-East Asia.

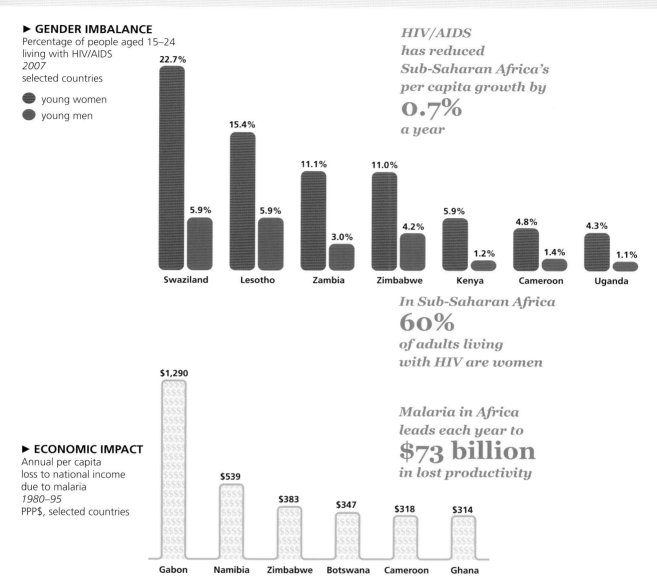

► GENDER IMBALANCE

Percentage of people aged 15–24 living with HIV/AIDS
2007
selected countries

● young women
● young men

22.7%	15.4%	11.1%	11.0%	5.9%	4.8%	4.3%
5.9%	5.9%	3.0%	4.2%	1.2%	1.4%	1.1%
Swaziland	Lesotho	Zambia	Zimbabwe	Kenya	Cameroon	Uganda

HIV/AIDS has reduced Sub-Saharan Africa's per capita growth by

0.7%

a year

In Sub-Saharan Africa

60%

of adults living with HIV are women

Malaria in Africa leads each year to

$73 billion

in lost productivity

► ECONOMIC IMPACT

Annual per capita loss to national income due to malaria
1980–95
PPP$, selected countries

$1,290	$539	$383	$347	$318	$314
Gabon	Namibia	Zimbabwe	Botswana	Cameroon	Ghana

Sub-Saharan Africa also has the highest incidence of tuberculosis (TB): 363 people per 100,000. Africa and Europe both experienced large increases in the incidence of TB during the 1990s, but globally the incidence has been gradually declining since 2004.

Around one-third of people living with HIV are also infected with TB – the cause of death for about half of people with AIDS. People who are HIV-positive and infected with TB are up to 40 times more likely to develop active TB than their compatriots who are not infected with HIV.

Despite recent progress, multidrug-resistant TB and HIV-associated TB plague some regions. About 1 in 20 new cases of TB – an estimated 0.5 million each year – are resistant to first-line drugs, with particularly high rates in Central Asia.

9.2 million
people were infected with TB and

1.7 million
people died from it in 2006

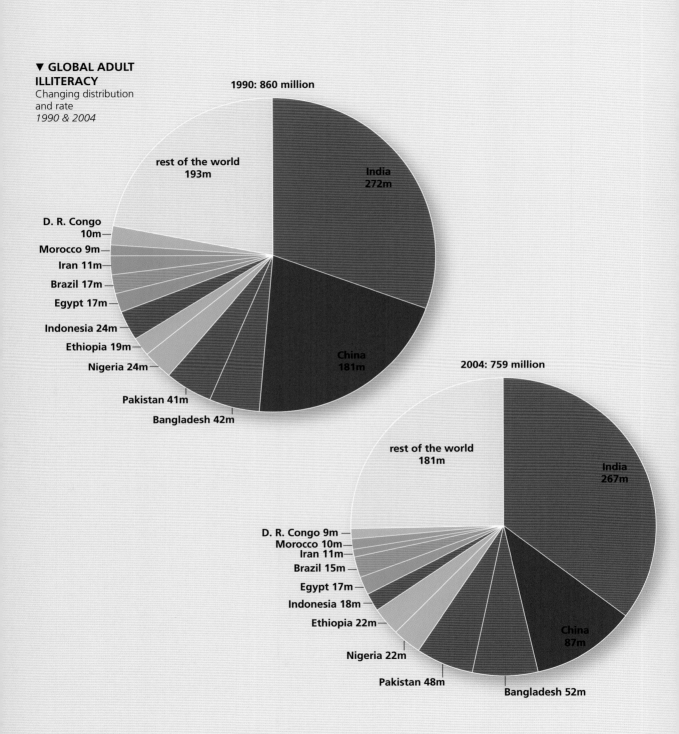

▼ **GLOBAL ADULT ILLITERACY**
Changing distribution and rate
1990 & 2004

1990: 860 million

rest of the world
193m

India
272m

D. R. Congo 10m
Morocco 9m
Iran 11m
Brazil 17m
Egypt 17m
Indonesia 24m
Ethiopia 19m
Nigeria 24m
Pakistan 41m
Bangladesh 42m

China
181m

2004: 759 million

rest of the world
181m

India
267m

D. R. Congo 9m
Morocco 10m
Iran 11m
Brazil 15m
Egypt 17m
Indonesia 18m
Ethiopia 22m
Nigeria 22m
Pakistan 48m
Bangladesh 52m

China
87m

Educational Inequalities 6

▶ The greatest benefit of education is that it empowers individuals with the essential tool of knowledge with which to enhance their lives with greater freedom and awareness. In April 2000, at a meeting in Dakar, Senegal, 164 countries adopted six goals related to education: literacy, universal primary education, early childhood care and education, the quality of that education, youth and adult learning, and gender equality. These goals provide a checklist for assessing progress towards Education for All.

Although the adult literacy rate has increased globally from 76 percent in 1990 to about 84 percent in 2007, literacy remains amongst the most neglected of all education goals, with 759 million adults lacking literacy skills today, almost two-thirds of whom are women.

The percentage of children enrolled in primary education is about 86 percent, and continues to rise, albeit very slowly. But while the number of children out of school has also dropped, from 105 million in 1999 to 72 million in 2007, the goal of achieving universal primary education by 2015 is unlikely to be met.

Early childhood care and education provides a firm basis for good outcomes in both health and education, and the benefits are normally long term. Yet, pre-primary gross enrolment ratios averaged only 36 percent in developing countries, compared with 79 percent in developed countries, and 175 million children entering primary school each year have experienced malnutrition, with all the developmental disadvantages this brings.

The quality of education offered continues to suffer in many low-income countries, with pupil–teacher ratios of 40:1, and many teachers not meeting the minimum standards.

The global economic crisis has resulted in high youth unemployment rates. Vocational education has remained ineffective in assisting youth employment in spite of investment in this sector, for example in the Middle East. Successful approaches to youth and adult learning may benefit from following the Brazilian model, in which the employers' federation is a major provider of high-quality training aimed at addressing labor-market shortages.

Deep-rooted inequalities linked to gender, wealth, ethnicity, language, and location are a major barrier to Education for All. Karamajong pastoralists in Uganda, Kurdish-speaking girls in Turkey, Hausa-speaking girls in Nigeria, and African-Americans in the USA all face a much higher risk of being left out of education.

Increased funding is needed at all levels of education. The share of GDP allocated to education remains at only 3 to 4 percent for several Sub-Saharan and South Asian countries. Although international aid to education has been rising, commitment fell by a fifth to $4.3 billion in 2007.

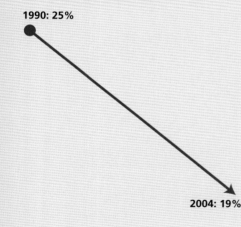

▼ ILLITERATE ADULTS AS PERCENTAGE OF TOTAL

1990: 25%

2004: 19%

Literacy

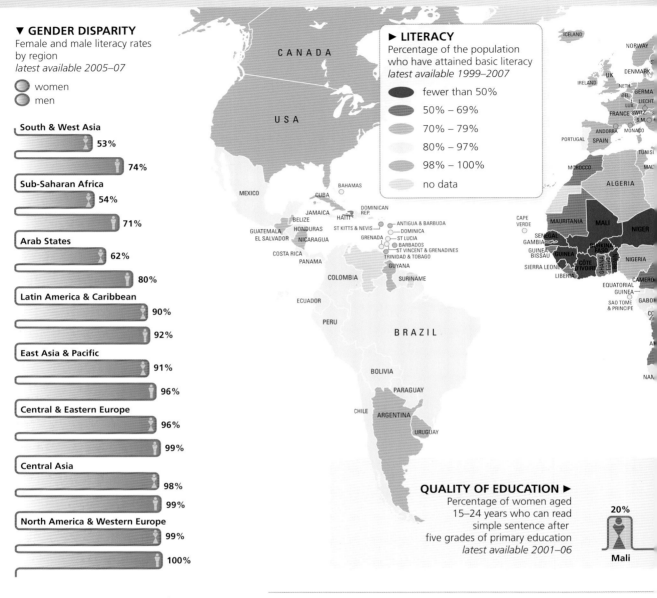

▼ GENDER DISPARITY
Female and male literacy rates by region
latest available 2005–07

⬤ women
⬤ men

South & West Asia
- 53%
- 74%

Sub-Saharan Africa
- 54%
- 71%

Arab States
- 62%
- 80%

Latin America & Caribbean
- 90%
- 92%

East Asia & Pacific
- 91%
- 96%

Central & Eastern Europe
- 96%
- 99%

Central Asia
- 98%
- 99%

North America & Western Europe
- 99%
- 100%

► LITERACY
Percentage of the population who have attained basic literacy
latest available 1999–2007

- fewer than 50%
- 50% – 69%
- 70% – 79%
- 80% – 97%
- 98% – 100%
- no data

QUALITY OF EDUCATION ►
Percentage of women aged 15–24 years who can read simple sentence after five grades of primary education
latest available 2001–06

20%
Mali

16%
of people are illiterate

35%
of illiterate people live in India

► Free, universal, elementary education is recognized as a human right in the Universal Declaration of Human Rights, adopted by the UN in 1948, and literacy is widely accepted as a catalyst for social development. Currently, 776 million adults lack fundamental literacy skills, and the majority live in the developing world.

Low literacy rates are clearly linked with poverty, both at a country level – the failure or inability of governments of poor countries to provide free education – and at the level of household income. There are marked inequalities between the educational opportunities open to the poorest and the better off citizens of developing-world countries. In Sub-Saharan Africa, for example, there are major disparities in primary school completion rates between those who can afford to send their children to

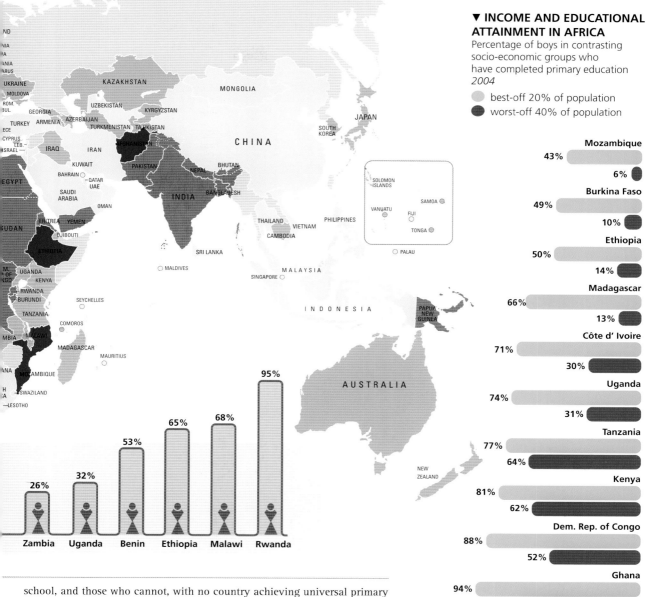

▼ INCOME AND EDUCATIONAL ATTAINMENT IN AFRICA

Percentage of boys in contrasting socio-economic groups who have completed primary education
2004

- ⬤ best-off 20% of population
- ⬤ worst-off 40% of population

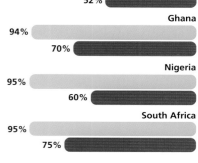

Mozambique
43%
6%

Burkina Faso
49%
10%

Ethiopia
50%
14%

Madagascar
66%
13%

Côte d' Ivoire
71%
30%

Uganda
74%
31%

Tanzania
77%
64%

Kenya
81%
62%

Dem. Rep. of Congo
88%
52%

Ghana
94%
70%

Nigeria
95%
60%

South Africa
95%
75%

school, and those who cannot, with no country achieving universal primary schooling for the poor.

Gender is a major factor in global illiteracy rates. Two-thirds of the world's illiterate people are women, and the three regions with the lowest literacy rates are those with the greatest gender disparities.

Quality of education is also a major determinant of literacy. The retained ability to read after having dropped out of primary school prior to completion is an important measure of the effectiveness of the schooling available. There are striking differences in the ability of young women across Sub-Saharan Africa to read a simple sentence.

Barriers to Education

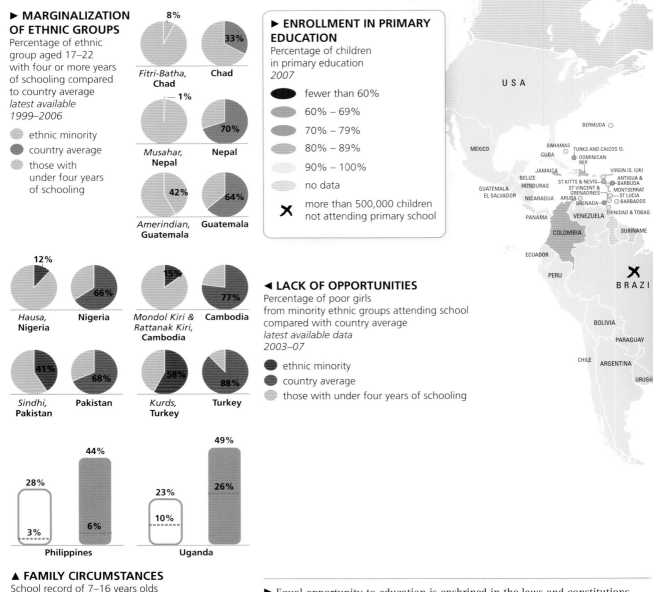

► MARGINALIZATION OF ETHNIC GROUPS

Percentage of ethnic group aged 17–22 with four or more years of schooling compared to country average
latest available
1999–2006

- ethnic minority
- country average
- those with under four years of schooling

8%
Fitri-Batha, Chad

33%
Chad

1%
Musahar, Nepal

70%
Nepal

42%
Amerindian, Guatemala

64%
Guatemala

12%
Hausa, Nigeria

66%
Nigeria

15%
Mondol Kiri & Rattanak Kiri, Cambodia

77%
Cambodia

41%
Sindhi, Pakistan

68%
Pakistan

58%
Kurds, Turkey

88%
Turkey

► ENROLLMENT IN PRIMARY EDUCATION

Percentage of children in primary education
2007

- fewer than 60%
- 60% – 69%
- 70% – 79%
- 80% – 89%
- 90% – 100%
- no data

✗ more than 500,000 children not attending primary school

◄ LACK OF OPPORTUNITIES

Percentage of poor girls from minority ethnic groups attending school compared with country average
latest available data
2003–07

- ethnic minority
- country average
- those with under four years of schooling

28%
44%

3%
6%
Philippines

23%
49%

10%
26%
Uganda

▲ FAMILY CIRCUMSTANCES

School record of 7–16 years olds with disabled parent from poorest fifth of population
2000–02

- - - country average
○ disadvantaged group who have never been to school
● disadvantaged group with fewer than four years education

► Equal opportunity to education is enshrined in the laws and constitutions of most countries. But, as UNESCO comments, "few human rights are more widely endorsed – and more widely violated". While most countries have accepted the goal of universal primary education, there are major disparities in access to primary education both between and within countries.

Education provides one of the most important escape routes from poverty, yet it is poverty, together with gender, ethnicity, language, location, and disability that most seriously limit access to even basic schooling. In many cases these factors combine to create multiple barriers. Some societies and governments seek to reduce this exclusion and discrimination. Many do not.

Minority ethnic groups are disadvantaged by both intolerance and the

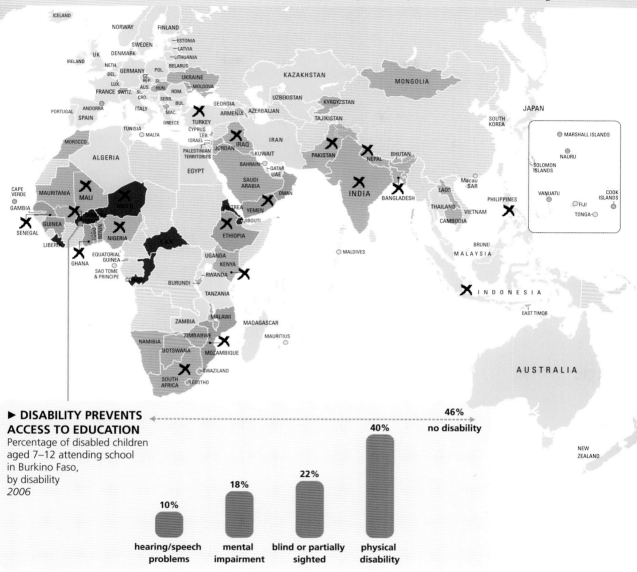

▶ **DISABILITY PREVENTS
ACCESS TO EDUCATION**
Percentage of disabled children
aged 7–12 attending school
in Burkino Faso,
by disability
2006

46% no disability

40% physical disability

22% blind or partially sighted

18% mental impairment

10% hearing/speech problems

lack of bilingual schooling. For example, in Nepal, virtually all of the Musahar people, doubly disadvantaged by ethnicity and caste, achieve fewer than four years of education while this is true for only 30 percent of the whole population. In many cases, lack of data makes it difficult to fully assess levels of deprivation. It is estimated that 30 percent of Roma children in Romania do not continue in school beyond the fourth grade, but information is scarce – privacy legislation in Romania prevents the collection of data on ethnicity, so this remains a hidden problem.

Disability is a major barrier to education. Schools often fail to address disabilities and may exacerbate the obstacles that disabled children face. Many schools are inaccessible or ill-equipped to meet the needs of disabled children, and segregated schooling may increase discrimination.

18%
*of children
of primary school age
in Vietnam are from ethnic
minorities compared with*
8% *of teachers*

Early Childhood Care & Education

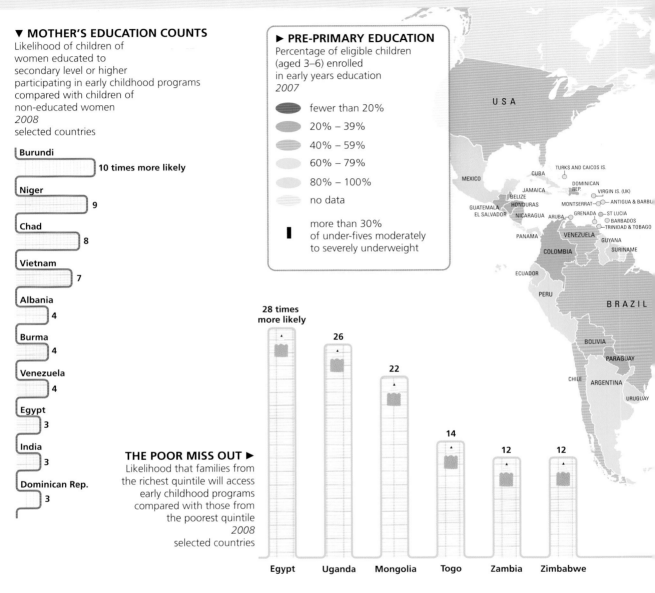

▼ MOTHER'S EDUCATION COUNTS

Likelihood of children of
women educated to
secondary level or higher
participating in early childhood programs
compared with children of
non-educated women
2008
selected countries

Burundi
10 times more likely

Niger
9

Chad
8

Vietnam
7

Albania
4

Burma
4

Venezuela
4

Egypt
3

India
3

Dominican Rep.
3

▶ PRE-PRIMARY EDUCATION

Percentage of eligible children
(aged 3–6) enrolled
in early years education
2007

- fewer than 20%
- 20% – 39%
- 40% – 59%
- 60% – 79%
- 80% – 100%
- no data

| more than 30%
of under-fives moderately
to severely underweight

USA

MEXICO
CUBA
TURKS AND CAICOS IS.
JAMAICA
DOMINICAN REP.
BELIZE
VIRGIN IS. (UK)
HONDURAS
ANTIGUA & BARBU
GUATEMALA
MONTSERRAT
EL SALVADOR
NICARAGUA
ARUBA
GRENADA
ST LUCIA
BARBADOS
TRINIDAD & TOBAGO
PANAMA
VENEZUELA
GUYANA
COLOMBIA
SURINAME

ECUADOR

PERU
BRAZIL

BOLIVIA
PARAGUAY
CHILE
ARGENTINA
URUGUAY

THE POOR MISS OUT ▶

Likelihood that families from
the richest quintile will access
early childhood programs
compared with those from
the poorest quintile
2008
selected countries

28 times more likely — Egypt
26 — Uganda
22 — Mongolia
14 — Togo
12 — Zambia
12 — Zimbabwe

Children in urban Burundi are

5 times

more likely than their rural counterparts to attend early childhood programs

▶ Children who are denied access to early childhood care and pre-school education suffer a range of health and educational disadvantages.

In developing countries, 15 percent of infants have a low birth weight, and almost 25 percent of children aged under five are sufficiently underweight to impair growth and development. Providing nutrition and healthcare at this early stage is critical, and has a long-term positive impact on overall well-being and attainment.

Early childhood education prepares children for primary school, and has been found to be an important factor in successful completion of high school education. However, poverty, the mother's lack of education, and living in a rural area all decrease the odds of a child participating in an early learning program.

Children who are denied access to early childhood care and pre-school education suffer a range of health and educational disadvantages.

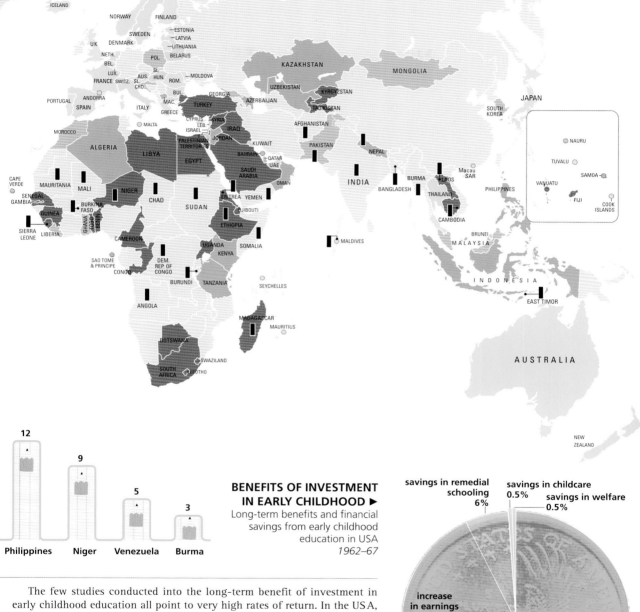

BENEFITS OF INVESTMENT IN EARLY CHILDHOOD ▶

Long-term benefits and financial savings from early childhood education in USA
1962–67

12	Philippines
9	Niger
5	Venezuela
3	Burma

The few studies conducted into the long-term benefit of investment in early childhood education all point to very high rates of return. In the USA, children who attended early childhood programs were shown to be much less likely to need remedial schooling, less likely to be engaged in crime as adults, less likely to be dependent on welfare, more likely to attend high school or college, and much more likely to have higher incomes. The result is a benefit–cost ratio of 17:1 for investment in early childhood education. This is a far higher ratio than benefit gained from investment in education later in a person's life.

Pre-school programs with parent participation can also play a key role in educating families, promoting the rights of children, providing pediatric health, and reducing child labor.

savings in remedial schooling 6%

savings in childcare 0.5%

savings in welfare 0.5%

increase in earnings 28%

savings in crime reduction 65%

Total benefits per child: $144,345

30.0 – 39.9	40.0 – 49.9	50.0 – 59.9	60.0 – 69.9	70.0 – 79.9
			26 Belize	
			27 Antigua & Barbuda	
			28 Singapore	
			29 Serbia & Mont.	
			30 Ecuador	
			31 Peru	
			32 Denmark	
			33 Hungary	
			34 El Salvador	
			35 Croatia	
			36 Dominican Rep.	
			37 Lithuania	
			38 Nepal	
			39 Suriname	
		79 Kyrgyzstan	40 Bhutan	
		80 Laos	41 Luxembourg	
		81 Namibia	42 Algeria	
		82 Guyana	43 Mexico	
		83 Uruguay	44 Ireland	
	118 Honduras	84 Azerbaijan	45 Romania	
	119 Uganda	85 Vietnam	46 Canada	
	120 Madagascar	86 Moldova	47 Netherlands	
	121 China	87 Ukraine	48 Maldives	
	122 Qatar	88 Belgium	49 Fiji	
	123 India	89 Jamaica	50 Philippines	
	124 Yemen	90 Lebanon	51 Australia	
	125 Pakistan	91 São Tome e Principe	52 Morocco	
	126 Tanzania	92 Kazakhstan	53 Belarus	
	127 Zimbabwe	93 Nicaragua	54 Malaysia	
	128 Burkina Faso	94 South Korea	55 Slovenia	
	129 Sudan	95 Gabon	56 Syria	
	130 Zambia	96 Cyprus	57 Estonia	
	131 Oman	97 Jordan	58 Sri Lanka	
	132 Guinea-Bissau	98 Bosnia & Herz.	59 Georgia	
	133 Cameroon	99 Saudi Arabia	60 Paraguay	7 France
	134 Indonesia	100 Eritrea	61 USA	8 Austria
	135 Rwanda	101 Swaziland	62 Brazil	9 Cuba
	136 Guinea	102 Côte d'Ivoire	63 Poland	10 Colombia
	137 Bolivia	103 Trinidad & Tobago	64 Venezuela	11 Malta
	138 Papua New Guinea	104 Guatemala	65 Bulgaria	12 Finland
	139 Bangladesh	105 Congo	66 Israel	13 Slovakia
	140 Burundi	106 Dem. Rep. Congo	67 Thailand	14 UK
	141 Ethiopia	107 Malawi	68 Egypt	15 New Zealand
	142 Mongolia	108 Kenya	69 Russia	16 Chile
	143 Senegal	109 Ghana	70 Argentina	17 Germany
154 Benin	144 Uzbekistan	110 Burma	71 Greece	18 Italy
155 Haiti	145 Bahrain	111 Tajikistan	72 Brunei	19 Portugal
156 Mali	146 Equatorial Guinea	112 Mozambique	73 Macedonia	20 Japan
157 Turkmenistan	147 North Korea	113 Kuwait	74 Tunisia	21 Latvia
158 Niger	148 Cambodia	114 Solomon Is.	75 Djibouti	22 Czech Rep.
159 Togo	149 Botswana	115 South Africa	76 Armenia	23 Albania
160 Angola	150 Iraq	116 Gambia	77 Turkey	24 Panama
161 Mauritania	151 Chad	117 Libya	78 Iran	25 Spain
162 Central African Rep.	152 U.A.E.			
163 Sierra Leone	153 Nigeria			

EPI SCORES

▶ Global awareness of significant environmental challenges grew in the second half of the 20th century. Controversy continues to surround what should be done and by which governments. Thus, what constitutes environmental justice and inequality remains debatable. This section captures significant environmental differences, mostly between nations, in climate, air pollution, water pollution and deforestation.

The Environmental Performance Index (EPI) is a recent, and also contentious, aggregate metric of progress. It measures the extent to which a country has met two core objectives: environmental health and ecosystem vitality. The index is a weighted measure of 25 indicators across 10 policy categories encompassing climate change, deforestation, air quality, water quality as well as fisheries, agriculture, and biodiversity.

The high EPI scores of industrialized countries reflect their strong performance in environmental health. In ecosystem vitality, by contrast, their performance varies. Some have high greenhouse gas emissions and rising levels of waste; many have agricultural subsidies promoting intense chemical use to the detriment of the environment.

The basic challenge of non-industrialized nations is still at the level of environmental health: access to safe drinking water and basic sanitation, deriving from poverty and under-investment in basic environmental amenities.

Statistical analysis shows that good governance as measured by the competence of the bureaucracy, the quality of policymaking, and public-service delivery contributes to better environmental outcomes and reduced inequalities. Examples include Costa Rica, a middle-income country ranked third in the world, which outperforms most developed countries, and Cuba, ranked ninth, with its strong environmental health scores and low levels of industrial pollution. Countries with high levels of corruption tend to have low levels of environmental performance, particularly in relation to environmental health and water quality.

The USA is ranked 61st out of 163 countries. This reflects its large contribution to global warming. The BRIC countries – Brazil, Russia, India, and China – occupy the ranks 62 (just behind the US) 69, 123, and 121 respectively, struggling with the pressures of large populations, rapidly growing industrial bases, and histories of pollution and resource mismanagement. However, countries with high population density are spread throughout the EPI, and high-ranked performers such as Singapore, El Salvador, and Nepal demonstrate that this is not an insurmountable barrier to good environmental quality.

The trend in access to improved water supplies was positive for most countries between 1990 to 2006 except for 15 countries, many of them the poorest, and some of them – Sierra Leone, Iraq, and occupied Palestinian Territories – locked in prolonged armed conflicts. Similarly, access to sanitation has also improved, except in notably unstable countries such as Liberia, Rwanda, and Haiti.

▼ INDICATORS
On which EPI is based

- environmental health
- ecosystem vitality

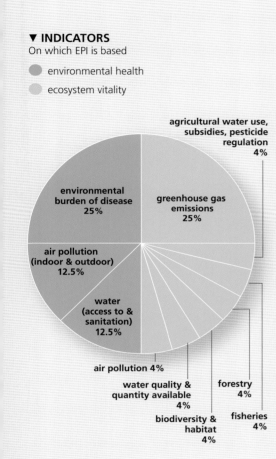

agricultural water use, subsidies, pesticide regulation 4%

greenhouse gas emissions 25%

environmental burden of disease 25%

air pollution (indoor & outdoor) 12.5%

water (access to & sanitation) 12.5%

air pollution 4%

water quality & quantity available 4%

biodiversity & habitat 4%

forestry 4%

fisheries 4%

1   Iceland
2   Switzerland
3   Costa Rica
4   Sweden
5   Norway
6   Mauritius

80.0 – 93.5

Climate Change

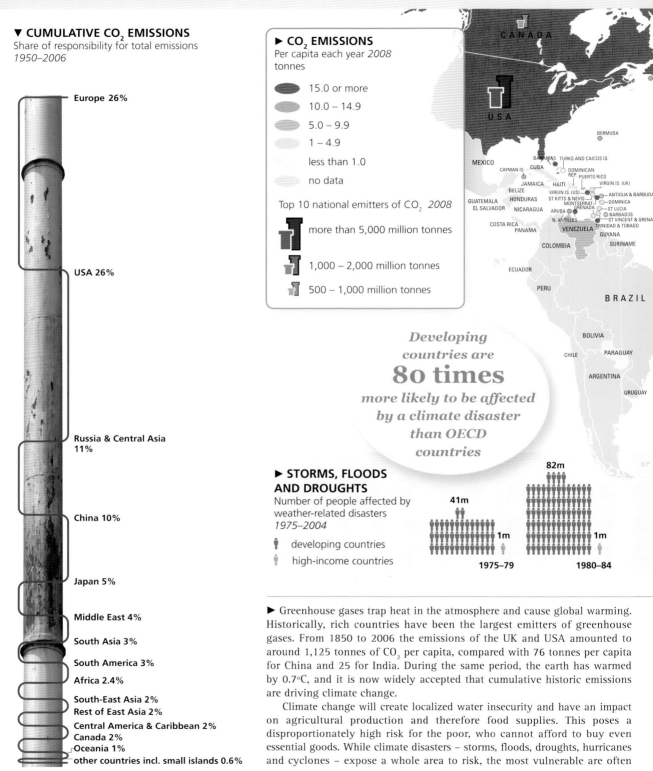

▼ CUMULATIVE CO₂ EMISSIONS
Share of responsibility for total emissions
1950–2006

- Europe 26%
- USA 26%
- Russia & Central Asia 11%
- China 10%
- Japan 5%
- Middle East 4%
- South Asia 3%
- South America 3%
- Africa 2.4%
- South-East Asia 2%
- Rest of East Asia 2%
- Central America & Caribbean 2%
- Canada 2%
- Oceania 1%
- other countries incl. small islands 0.6%

► CO₂ EMISSIONS
Per capita each year *2008*
tonnes

- 15.0 or more
- 10.0 – 14.9
- 5.0 – 9.9
- 1 – 4.9
- less than 1.0
- no data

Top 10 national emitters of CO₂ *2008*

- more than 5,000 million tonnes
- 1,000 – 2,000 million tonnes
- 500 – 1,000 million tonnes

Developing countries are **80 times** *more likely to be affected by a climate disaster than OECD countries*

► STORMS, FLOODS AND DROUGHTS
Number of people affected by weather-related disasters
1975–2004

- developing countries
- high-income countries

82m
41m
1m 1m

1975–79   1980–84

► Greenhouse gases trap heat in the atmosphere and cause global warming. Historically, rich countries have been the largest emitters of greenhouse gases. From 1850 to 2006 the emissions of the UK and USA amounted to around 1,125 tonnes of CO₂ per capita, compared with 76 tonnes per capita for China and 25 for India. During the same period, the earth has warmed by 0.7°C, and it is now widely accepted that cumulative historic emissions are driving climate change.

Climate change will create localized water insecurity and have an impact on agricultural production and therefore food supplies. This poses a disproportionately high risk for the poor, who cannot afford to buy even essential goods. While climate disasters – storms, floods, droughts, hurricanes and cyclones – expose a whole area to risk, the most vulnerable are often

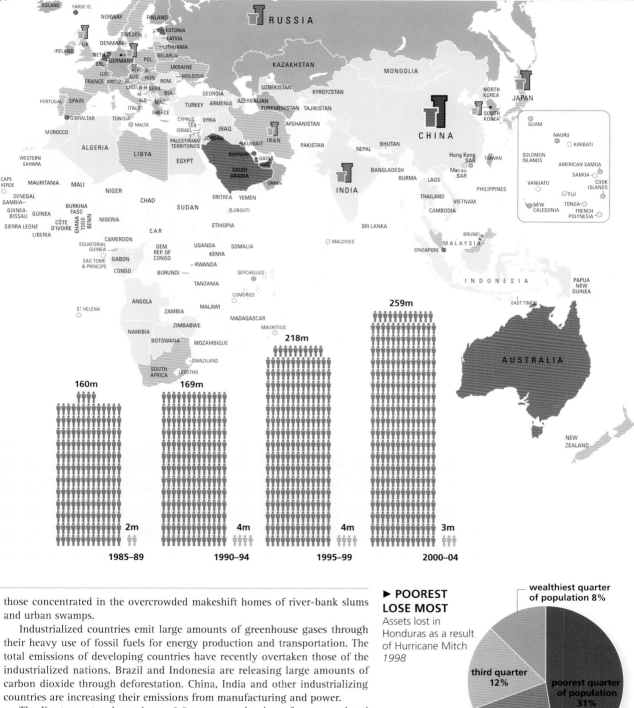

Industrialized countries have historically been the largest carbon emitters, but developing nations and the poor bear the brunt of the resultant climate disasters.

160m
1985–89
2m

169m
1990–94
4m

218m
1995–99
4m

259m
2000–04
3m

those concentrated in the overcrowded makeshift homes of river-bank slums and urban swamps.

Industrialized countries emit large amounts of greenhouse gases through their heavy use of fossil fuels for energy production and transportation. The total emissions of developing countries have recently overtaken those of the industrialized nations. Brazil and Indonesia are releasing large amounts of carbon dioxide through deforestation. China, India and other industrializing countries are increasing their emissions from manufacturing and power.

The Kyoto protocol requires a 2.5 percent reduction of energy-related CO_2 emissions in real terms by the 2010/12 target date. However, several developed nations, including the USA, Australia, Canada, Spain, Italy, and Japan, remain far short of this target.

▶ **POOREST LOSE MOST**
Assets lost in Honduras as a result of Hurricane Mitch *1998*

wealthiest quarter of population 8%

third quarter 12%

poorest quarter of population 31%

second quarter 14%

Deforestation

MAIN CAUSES OF DEFORESTATION

Latin America
- policies facilitating land transfer to large, private ranches
- state policy of colonization, leading to inward migration by poor settlers
- road construction followed by slash-and-burn agriculture
- pasture-creation for cattle ranching

West & Central Africa
- weak law enforcement
- inward migration and rapid population growth
- private timber logging, often by foreign firms

South-East Asia
- policies facilitating colonization, state plantations and large transmigration projects
- corruption and weak law enforcement
- insecure land ownership
- private and state-run commercial timber logging
- slash-and-burn and agriculture and permanent plantations

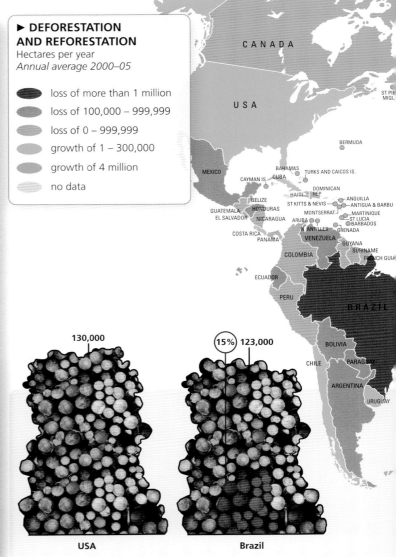

▶ **DEFORESTATION AND REFORESTATION**
Hectares per year
Annual average 2000–05

- loss of more than 1 million
- loss of 100,000 – 999,999
- loss of 0 – 999,999
- growth of 1 – 300,000
- growth of 4 million
- no data

130,000

15% 123,000

USA

Brazil

60 million
indigenous people depend completely on forests;
350 million
people depend heavily on forests

▶ Humans depend on forests for a wide variety of vital resources, including food, fuel, medicine, clean water, and clean air. Forested areas make up roughly 26 percent of the Earth's land surface, but deforestation, particularly in Brazil, Indonesia, and tropical Africa, is shrinking this area. In some parts of the globe, reforestation is occurring.

Deforestation is caused by complex chains of factors that vary around the world. They include timber logging by private, foreign, or state-run companies, road building allowing new settlement, and agricultural expansion. Deforestation is also caused by natural disasters such as fires, droughts, floods, and pests. Carbon, locked up in forests, is released during deforestation, contributing around 17 percent of global emissions.

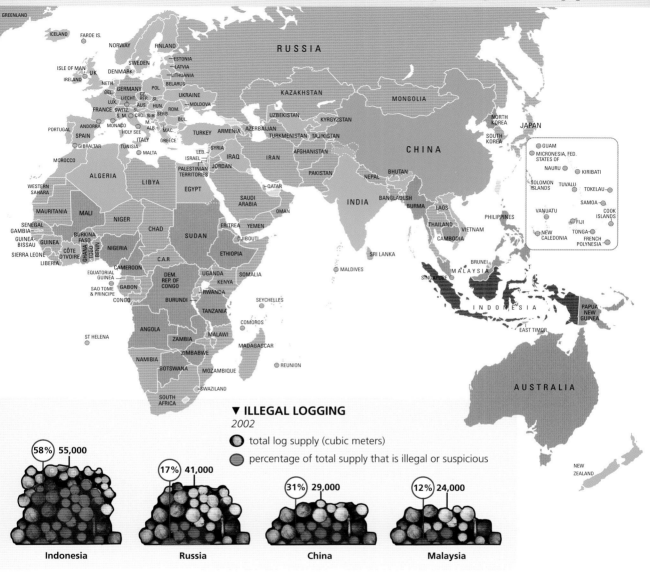

▼ **ILLEGAL LOGGING**
2002

total log supply (cubic meters)

percentage of total supply that is illegal or suspicious

58% 55,000	**17%** 41,000	**31%** 29,000	**12%** 24,000
Indonesia	**Russia**	**China**	**Malaysia**

Underlying driving forces of deforestation include economic, technological, political, cultural, and demographic factors. Indigenous people are losing their historic rights to forest areas. Women may be disproportionately affected because their rights are particularly weak and they bear the burden of collecting increasingly scarce food, fuel, and water.

Several case studies have shown that the economic gains associated with deforestation are typically low, and well-designed policy and market incentives can reduce deforestation significantly. To be effective, however, incentives will have to influence both the influential state and private actors, as well as the many millions of farmers whose actions drive land-use changes in the tropical forest margins.

Brazil and Indonesia accounted for **68%** *of the world's deforestation 2000–05*

Air Pollution & Health

800,000 children *younger than five die each year of pneumonia related to indoor air pollution*

▲ DISEASE AND DEATH

Disability Adjusted Life Years lost to indoor air pollution from solid fuel use
2004
Annual DALYs per 1,000 people

- more than 60
- 31 – 60
- 11 – 30
- 1 – 10
- fewer than 1
- no data

Deaths due to indoor air pollution
2004

- more than 100,000 deaths
- 20,000 – 100,000 deaths

A Disability Adjusted Life Year (DALY) is the equivalent of one year of healthy life lost due to illness and disability.

dung 720 · 365 · 100
wood 500 · 345 · 97
kerosene 205 · 297 · 0

► Air pollution can cause both illness and death. A particularly widespread problem is the pollution of air inside homes from the burning of solid fuels on open fires by people who lack an alternative method of cooking or of keeping warm. Women and children are disproportionately affected because women do most of the cooking, and children accompany their mothers.

The burning of fuels releases toxic gases – including carbon monoxide, nitrous oxides, and sulfur oxides – and small particles that enter the respiratory system. If these are not efficiently removed by means of a chimney they can cause a range of illnesses, including pneumonia and cancer. It is estimated that the years of healthy life lost to illness and disability caused by indoor air pollution represent 2.7 percent of the global burden of disease.

Air pollution, both indoors and outdoors, is a significant cause of death and disabling disease.

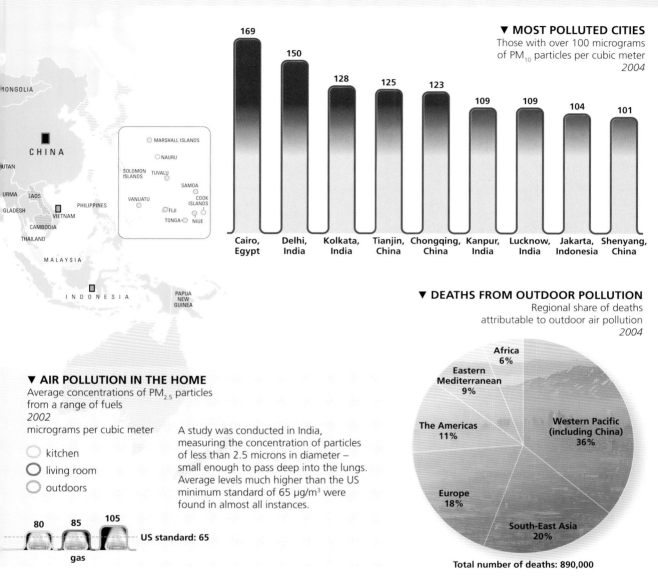

▼ MOST POLLUTED CITIES
Those with over 100 micrograms of PM$_{10}$ particles per cubic meter
2004

Cairo, Egypt	Delhi, India	Kolkata, India	Tianjin, China	Chongqing, China	Kanpur, India	Lucknow, India	Jakarta, Indonesia	Shenyang, China
169	150	128	125	123	109	109	104	101

▼ DEATHS FROM OUTDOOR POLLUTION
Regional share of deaths attributable to outdoor air pollution
2004

- Africa 6%
- Eastern Mediterranean 9%
- The Americas 11%
- Europe 18%
- South-East Asia 20%
- Western Pacific (including China) 36%

Total number of deaths: 890,000

▼ AIR POLLUTION IN THE HOME
Average concentrations of PM$_{2.5}$ particles from a range of fuels
2002
micrograms per cubic meter

- ○ kitchen
- ○ living room
- ○ outdoors

A study was conducted in India, measuring the concentration of particles of less than 2.5 microns in diameter – small enough to pass deep into the lungs. Average levels much higher than the US minimum standard of 65 µg/m³ were found in almost all instances.

80   85   105
US standard: 65

gas

Another cause of indoor air pollution is tobacco smoke. Someone breathing in "second-hand" smoke is exposed to the same toxic components as a smoker, albeit in different relative amounts. Even short-term exposure to such smoke can increase the risk of coronary disease and cause premature death.

Outdoor air pollution can also be a significant health threat, especially in urban areas. Most air pollutants released outdoors originate from the combustion of fossil fuels such as coal or oil for transportation or power generation.

To reduce the health impact of air pollution, cleaner energy sources will be needed. This, however, will often require investment in power infrastructure, particularly in rural areas.

Urban air pollution caused
800,000
deaths
and nearly
8 million
years lost to disability in 2002

Water & Health

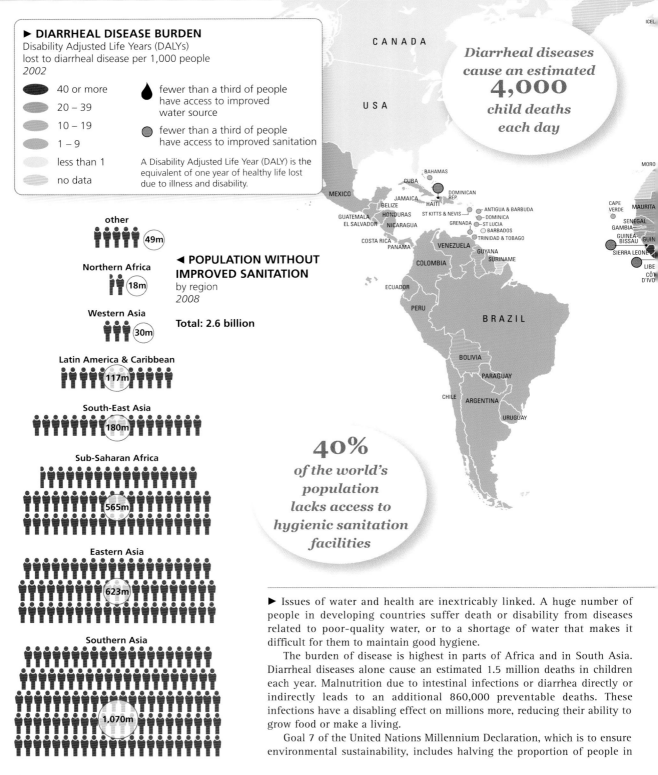

▶ DIARRHEAL DISEASE BURDEN

Disability Adjusted Life Years (DALYs)
lost to diarrheal disease per 1,000 people
2002

- 40 or more
- 20 – 39
- 10 – 19
- 1 – 9
- less than 1
- no data

💧 fewer than a third of people have access to improved water source

⬤ fewer than a third of people have access to improved sanitation

A Disability Adjusted Life Year (DALY) is the equivalent of one year of healthy life lost due to illness and disability.

◀ POPULATION WITHOUT IMPROVED SANITATION
by region
2008

Total: 2.6 billion

- other — 49m
- Northern Africa — 18m
- Western Asia — 30m
- Latin America & Caribbean — 117m
- South-East Asia — 180m
- Sub-Saharan Africa — 565m
- Eastern Asia — 623m
- Southern Asia — 1,070m

Diarrheal diseases cause an estimated **4,000** *child deaths each day*

40% *of the world's population lacks access to hygienic sanitation facilities*

▶ Issues of water and health are inextricably linked. A huge number of people in developing countries suffer death or disability from diseases related to poor-quality water, or to a shortage of water that makes it difficult for them to maintain good hygiene.

The burden of disease is highest in parts of Africa and in South Asia. Diarrheal diseases alone cause an estimated 1.5 million deaths in children each year. Malnutrition due to intestinal infections or diarrhea directly or indirectly leads to an additional 860,000 preventable deaths. These infections have a disabling effect on millions more, reducing their ability to grow food or make a living.

Goal 7 of the United Nations Millennium Declaration, which is to ensure environmental sustainability, includes halving the proportion of people in

A tenth of all disease could be alleviated by improvements in household water, sanitation, and water-resource management. The poor are most likely to lack clean water and sanitation services.

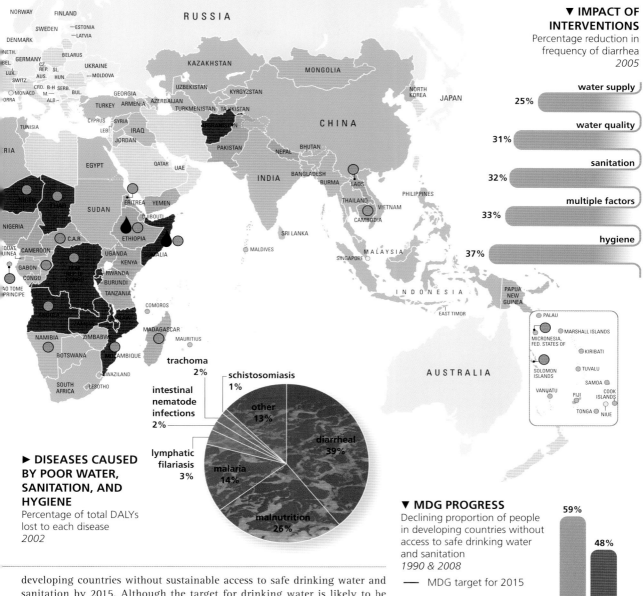

▼ IMPACT OF INTERVENTIONS
Percentage reduction in frequency of diarrhea
2005

water supply
25%

water quality
31%

sanitation
32%

multiple factors
33%

hygiene
37%

► DISEASES CAUSED BY POOR WATER, SANITATION, AND HYGIENE
Percentage of total DALYs lost to each disease
2002

trachoma 2%
schistosomiasis 1%
intestinal nematode infections 2%
lymphatic filariasis 3%
other 13%
diarrheal 39%
malaria 14%
malnutrition 26%

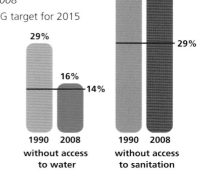

▼ MDG PROGRESS
Declining proportion of people in developing countries without access to safe drinking water and sanitation
1990 & 2008

— MDG target for 2015

without access to water
1990: 29%
2008: 16%
14%

without access to sanitation
1990: 59%
2008: 48%
29%

developing countries without sustainable access to safe drinking water and sanitation by 2015. Although the target for drinking water is likely to be reached, because of increasing populations in the countries most affected the number without access remained, in 2008, at nearly 900 million. The target for sanitation is proving more difficult to reach, and 2.6 billion people still lacked access to hygienic toilet facilities in 2008.

The World Health Organization estimates that 10 percent of the total global burden of disease could be alleviated by access to safe water sources and sanitation facilities. These need to be backed up by better management of water resources, including the safe treatment of sewage. However, simple hygiene interventions, such as the promotion of hand-washing, have proved effective.

95

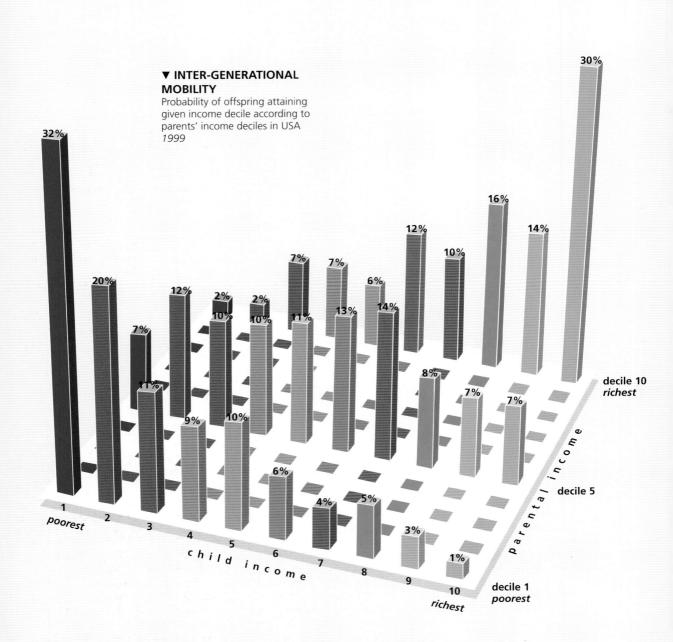

▼ **INTER-GENERATIONAL MOBILITY**
Probability of offspring attaining given income decile according to parents' income deciles in USA
1999

Towards Equality 8

At least one opinion poll suggests that 70 percent of Americans believe "personal attributes, like hard work and drive, are more important to economic mobility than external conditions," and that the majority believe that "it is more important to give people a fair chance to succeed than it is to reduce inequality in this country." (Pew Foundation, 2010) Further research shows that those Americans who believe that hard work or willingness to take risks leads to success oppose redistributive programs from rich to poor. Conversely, those who think that inheritance, family environment, and knowing the right people, provide the keys to success support equality-enhancing redistributive programs

Assuming no international migration, at least 80 percent of variability in the income of the nearly 7 billion people in the world can solely be explained by two characteristics determined at birth: country of citizenship, and parental income class within that country. Research on inter-generational mobility in the USA has shown that there is significant correlation between parents' and children's income deciles across generations, and that there is very little mobility, particularly at the bottom and the top income deciles (see graphic left).

Addressing inequality

Four broad processes that cause and perpetuate inequality were outlined in the Introduction (pages 9–13): distantiation, exploitation, exclusion, and hierarchy. Social movements to resist these forms of inequality have sometimes brought historic change. Labor movements in many parts of the world have fought exploitation and distantiation. Partly in response, redistributive taxation is common, particularly in industrial Europe, but remains episodically controversial. The civil rights movement resisted racial exclusion in the USA, as did the anti-apartheid struggle in South Africa. The feminist movement has advanced women's inclusion in the work force. Established hierarchies within corporations, churches, government, and society have occasionally been flattened in response to a range of goals and pressures.

State action on inequality

In some countries, bold and decisive action, particularly after wars and during crises, has brought historic social innovations. After the Chinese revolution in1949, land reforms, barefoot village doctors, and guarantees of employment and food, brought longer life expectancy and lower infant mortality. In 1930s USA, the New Deal brought relief to the unemployed, recovery to rebuild the economy, and reform of finance. In the process, it brought broad reductions in many dimensions of inequality. During and after the Second World War, state action brought healthcare and the welfare state to the UK and expanded it elsewhere in Europe, reducing inequality and vulnerability to risks of ill-health and unemployment.

Such state actions can be achieved with, and without, economic growth. Costa Rica, where industrial growth has not been strong, expanded welfare support, reduced child morality, and raised life expectancy to levels characteristic of much wealthier countries by 1980. In South Korea, from the 1960s onwards, flexible state guidance of industry, selective engagement with the world economy and favorable conditions, enabled the expansion of industrial production and skills. Land reform of the 1950s had resulted in a relatively equal distribution of land, and growth was comparatively equitable because it focused on labor-intensive industries. From the late 1970s, as authoritarian rule declined, there was marked expansion of expenditure on health, education and social security. The combination of increased incomes from industrial wages and state action raised living standards, and reduced child mortality in South Korea from levels characteristic of many developing countries in the 1950s to those of the industrialized world by the late 1980s.

International action

At the international level, the repertoire of action is limited, and achieving the goal of equality may require more creativity. Two main types of action have engaged with inter-country distantiation: foreign aid and national attempts to catch up economically through industrialization. Foreign aid has occasionally been cast as reparations

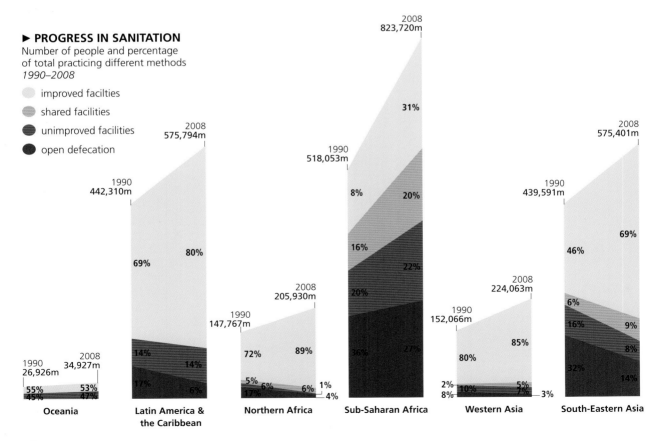

▶ **PROGRESS IN SANITATION**
Number of people and percentage of total practicing different methods
1990–2008

- improved facilties
- shared facilities
- unimproved facilities
- open defecation

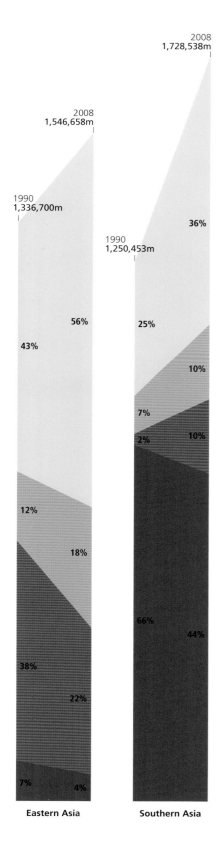

2008
1,728,538m

2008
1,546,658m

1990
1,336,700m

1990
1,250,453m

36%

56%   25%

43%

10%

7%

2%   10%

12%

18%

66%

44%

38%

22%

7%   4%

Eastern Asia   **Southern Asia**

for the wrongs of colonialism and slavery, but it is popular and on a significant scale from only a few industrial countries. Economic growth and industrialization are central to discussions of development, and have been discussed throughout the pages of this atlas.

Calls for international action to recognize temporary labor migration, to introduce global institutions to support human security, and to tax destabilizing financial flows may gain increasing support in future, particularly with the rise of the new international powers: Brazil, Russia, India, and China (BRIC). Strangely, coordinated global action to support new forms of employment-creating and inequality-reducing trade have not been suggested as a response to the ongoing global recession. Although economic aid and targeted actions can assist the poor, international practices in trade and lending need to change in order to make a larger impact. Global inequalities in power are reflected in the international decision-making bodies such as the World Trade Organization (WTO), the IMF and World Bank, where the framing of decisions may have a far-reaching impact on inequalities.

Significant progress has been made on several fronts, exemplified by the Millennium Development Goals, and inequalities have been reduced in many areas. Some inequalities, sanitation among them, seem, however, intractable (see graphic). Open defecation, with its health risks, threat to dignity and risk of assault against women, remains common in South Asia and Sub-Saharan Africa, largely because there is little money to be made, and limited political advantage to be gained, from sanitation. But a community-led movement for sanitation is gradually making progress in many countries.

Much remains to be done

If we return to the formulation of equality with which we opened this atlas, it is clear that much remains to be done. *Each person should have comparable freedoms across a range of dimensions*: inequality remains in many dimensions – women's subordination, literacy, nourishment, mobility, security, flourishing of children. *There is substantial global consensus that deprivations below a range of achievements are unacceptable*: hunger, income poverty, maternal mortality, barriers to education, open defecation, and much else, require action.

▼ **UNREGISTERED BIRTHS**
Number of children
born and not registered
2007

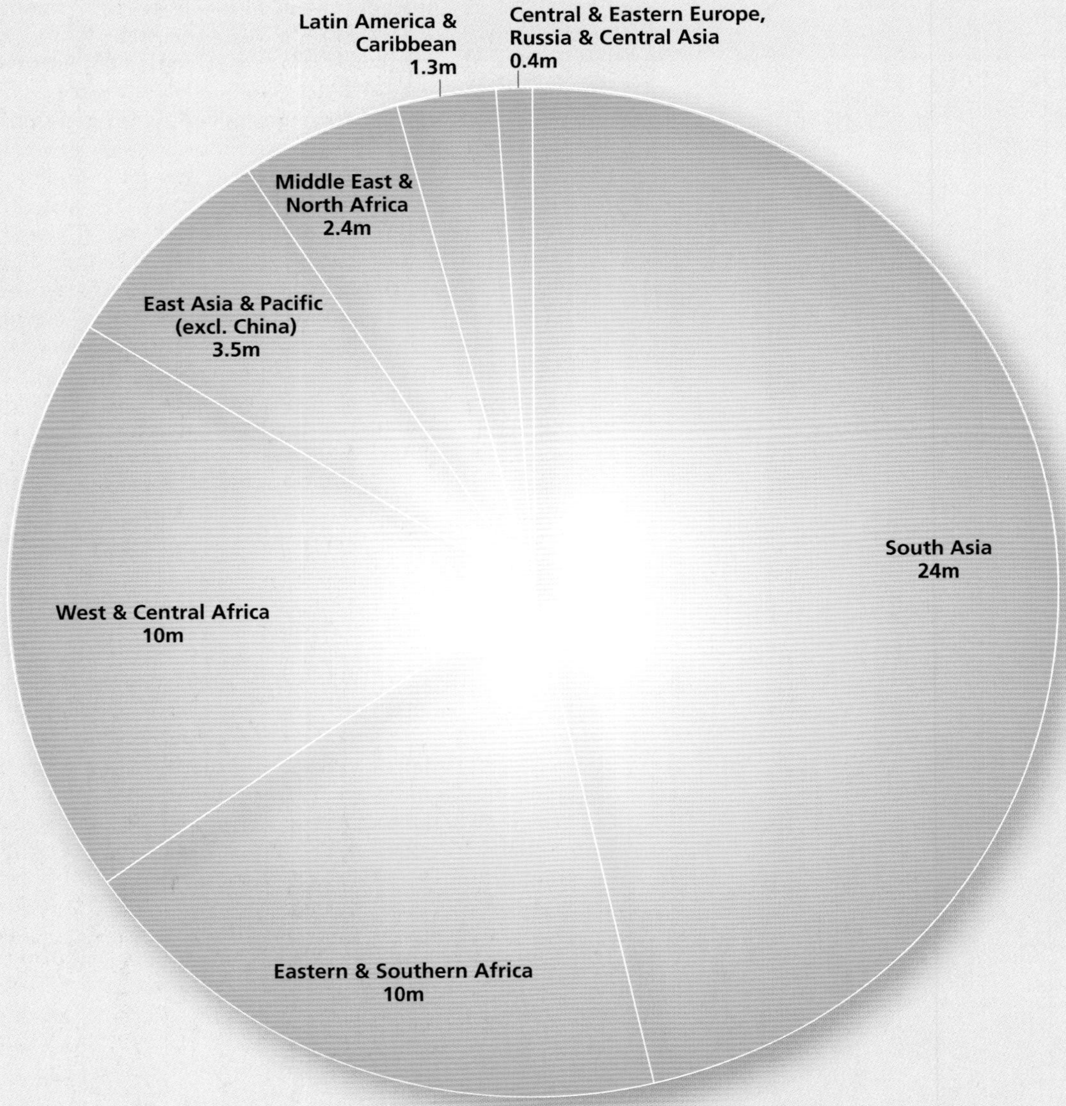

**Latin America &
Caribbean
1.3m**

**Central & Eastern Europe,
Russia & Central Asia
0.4m**

**Middle East &
North Africa
2.4m**

**East Asia & Pacific
(excl. China)
3.5m**

**South Asia
24m**

**West & Central Africa
10m**

**Eastern & Southern Africa
10m**

Total: 51 million

Data, Definitions & Sources 9

▶ There are a series of challenges in the collection and interpretation of data on global inequalities. One is registering the birth of a child. Although birth registration is considered a fundamental human right under the UN Convention on the Rights of the Child (1989), around 51 million children (excluding those in China) born in 2007 were not registered. These children are thus invisible to the state, and may be beyond the reach of the protection and services to which they have a right.

Most global data are collected by statistical bureaux of national governments, and aggregated by international agencies. Significant differences in data collection methods and questions asked makes this task difficult. Gradually, however, international collaborations are providing more consistent data. For example, since 1984 a series of Demographic and Health Surveys, with backing from USAID, has reached 84 countries nearly every year. Since the mid-1990s, UNICEF has been providing assistance for surveys focused on the condition of children. But, despite progress toward more reliable and comparable data collection, key challenges remain. These include questions of conceptualization, implementation and, not least, omission.

Conceptualization: How should we measure the freedoms, needs, and capabilities of individuals? Is $1.25 a day an adequate measure of poverty? If poverty is conceptualized as exclusion from a desired life, or as the experience of oppression, then the ability to purchase goods is only part of the story.

Implementation: Non-monetized activity, including domestic work, mostly done by women, agriculture for direct consumption, unpaid or informal sector work, are all more difficult to count than monetized activities.

Omissions: Statistical agencies tend not to collect data that reflects badly upon their masters, unless prompted by citizen or international action. They tend not to ask questions about the work women do collecting water and fuel and maintaining the home, about homelessness, corruption, and much else. Corporations often fail to report on the wages and conditions of low-paid workers, the top salaries of corporate executives, and the social disruption and toxic releases caused by their operations. Data about global flows, other than those of finance and trade, are collected erratically, largely by non-profit agencies.

The use of quantitative data, while it is often represented as an indication of rigor, makes no sense without analysis of the social processes of which it is a part. So, detailed cases, histories, and social science analyses – qualitative exploration – is required before numbers make sense. The synthesis of qualitative analysis and quantitative data can be used as an effective tool for policy making, monitoring progress, and holding decision-makers accountable.

Income, Expenditure, & Earnings

	Total population millions 2008	GNI per capita PPP$ 2008 or latest available	Gini index latest available 1995–2004	Wealth per household PPP$ 2000	Human Development Index score 2007
Afghanistan	29.0	1,100	–	–	0.352
Albania	3.1	7,520	31	10,574	0.818
Algeria	34.4	7,890	35	7,320	0.754
Angola	18.0	4,830	–	–	0.564
Antigua & Barbuda	0.1	19,660	–	20,944	0.868
Argentina	39.9	14,000	51	36,740	0.866
Armenia	3.1	6,310	34	9,480	0.798
Australia	21.4	37,250	–	90,906	0.970
Austria	8.3	37,360	29	73,047	0.955
Azerbaijan	8.7	7,770	37	6,737	0.787
Bahamas	0.3	–	–	–	0.856
Bahrain	0.8	33,430	–	–	0.895
Bangladesh	160.0	1,450	33	6,305	0.543
Barbados	0.3	18,240	–	102,932	0.903
Belarus	9.7	12,120	30	14,659	0.826
Belgium	10.7	35,380	33	86,205	0.953
Belize	0.3	5,940	–	12,550	0.772
Benin	8.7	1,470	37	3,378	0.492
Bhutan	0.7	4,820	–	–	0.619
Bolivia	9.7	4,140	60	6,654	0.729
Bosnia & Herzegovina	3.8	8,360	26	–	0.812
Botswana	1.9	13,310	–	15,719	0.694
Brazil	192.0	10,080	57	19,676	0.813
Brunei	0.4	50,820	–	–	0.920
Bulgaria	7.6	11,370	29	15,120	0.840
Burkina Faso	15.2	1,160	40	2,123	0.389
Burma	49.6	1,020	–	–	0.586
Burundi	8.1	380	42	1,876	0.394
Cambodia	14.6	1,870	42	4,890	0.593
Cameroon	19.1	2,170	45	5,290	0.523
Canada	33.3	38,710	33	89,252	0.966
Cape Verde	0.5	3,090	–	10,801	0.708
Central African Republic	4.3	730	–	1,949	0.369
Chad	10.9	1,070	–	1,726	0.392
Chile	16.8	13,250	55	27,536	0.878
China	1,324.7	6,010	47	11,267	0.772
Colombia	45.0	8,430	59	13,826	0.807
Comoros	0.6	1,170	–	5,182	0.576
Congo	3.6	2,810	–	2,806	0.601
Congo, Dem. Rep.	64.3	280	–	1,400	0.389
Cook Islands	0.01	–	–	–	–
Costa Rica	4.5	10,960	50	14,718	0.854
Côte d'Ivoire	20.6	1,580	45	5,212	0.484
Croatia	4.4	17,050	29	22,021	0.871
Cuba	11.2	–	–	–	0.863
Cyprus	0.9	24,980	–	–	0.914
Czech Republic	10.4	22,890	25	32,431	0.903
Denmark	5.5	37,530	25	66,191	0.955

Food expenditure as % of household expenditure on consumables *latest available 1998–2008*	Military expenditure as % of spending on healthcare and education *2007–08*	National minimum wage as % of GDP per capita *2008–09*	Healthcare % of total healthcare that is privately funded *2006*	Child labor % of 5–14 year olds working disproportionate hours *1999–2007*	
–	–	113%	67%	30%	Afghanistan
68%	34%	60%	62%	12%	Albania
53%	79%	46%	18%	5%	Algeria
–	–	28%	13%	24%	Angola
–	–	43%	32%	–	Antigua & Barbuda
33%	–	57%	54%	7%	Argentina
54%	60%	29%	58%	4%	Armenia
20%	17%	51%	32%	–	Australia
20%	7%	35%	24%	–	Austria
60%	114%	16%	74%	7%	Azerbaijan
27%	12%	38%	50%	5%	Bahamas
–	–	–	31%	–	Bahrain
54%	32%	61%	68%	13%	Bangladesh
–	8%	39%	36%	–	Barbados
42%	13%	20%	24%	5%	Belarus
16%	8%	52%	27%	–	Belgium
–	13%	68%	45%	40%	Belize
–	17%	98%	49%	46%	Benin
39%	–	30%	28%	19%	Bhutan
–	16%	55%	37%	22%	Bolivia
35%	–	62%	44%	5%	Bosnia & Herzegovina
–	23%	19%	23%	–	Botswana
21%	18%	37%	51%	6%	Brazil
–	69%	–	19%	–	Brunei
50%	31%	33%	42%	–	Bulgaria
49%	16%	143%	42%	47%	Burkina Faso
70%	84%	35%	84%	–	Burma
–	62%	24%	86%	19%	Burundi
71%	35%	33%	74%	45%	Cambodia
–	32%	63%	78%	31%	Cameroon
18%	10%	41%	30%	–	Canada
41%	5%	56%	20%	3%	Cape Verde
58%	39%	50%	59%	47%	Central African Republic
58%	24%	87%	45%	53%	Chad
23%	55%	37%	46%	3%	Chile
40%	–	–	59%	–	China
–	39%	56%	14%	5%	Colombia
–	–	132%	45%	27%	Comoros
–	45%	49%	28%	25%	Congo
–	–	125%	79%	32%	Congo, Dem. Rep.
–	–	–	7%	–	Cook Islands
31%	–	37%	31%	5%	Costa Rica
–	27%	87%	75%	35%	Côte d'Ivoire
30%	17%	43%	13%	–	Croatia
–	–	60%	4%	–	Cuba
15%	19%	40%	54%	–	Cyprus
27%	13%	27%	9%	–	Czech Republic
17%	8%	61%	14%	–	Denmark

Income, Expenditure, & Earnings

	Total population millions 2008	GNI per capita PPP$ 2008 or latest available	Gini index latest available 1995–2004	Wealth per household PPP$ 2000	Human Development Index score 2007
Djibouti	0.8	2,320	–	–	0.520
Dominica	0.1	8,300	–	12,717	0.814
Dominican Republic	10.0	7,800	52	13,873	0.777
East Timor	1.1	4,690	–	–	0.489
Ecuador	13.5	7,780	54	6,758	0.806
Egypt	81.5	5,470	34	15,541	0.703
El Salvador	6.1	6,630	52	18,408	0.747
Equatorial Guinea	0.7	21,720	–	7,404	0.719
Eritrea	4.9	640	–	–	0.472
Estonia	1.3	19,320	36	24,556	0.883
Ethiopia	80.7	870	30	1,412	0.414
Fiji	0.8	4,320	–	9,928	0.741
Finland	5.3	35,940	27	53,154	0.959
France	62.3	33,280	33	94,557	0.961
Gabon	1.4	12,400	–	14,833	0.755
Gambia	1.7	1,280	50	3,894	0.456
Georgia	4.3	4,920	40	13,258	0.778
Germany	82.1	35,950	28	90,768	0.947
Ghana	23.4	1,320	41	3,903	0.526
Greece	11.2	28,300	34	69,855	0.942
Grenada	0.1	8,430	–	15,250	0.813
Guatemala	13.7	4,690	55	12,858	0.704
Guinea	9.8	970	39	7,756	0.435
Guinea–Bissau	1.6	520	–	1,673	0.396
Guyana	0.8	3,030	–	5,697	0.729
Haiti	9.9	–	59	6,244	0.532
Honduras	7.3	3,830	54	5,318	0.732
Hungary	10.0	18,210	27	31,452	0.879
Iceland	0.3	25,300	–	81,945	0.969
India	1,140.0	2,930	37	6,513	0.612
Indonesia	227.3	3,600	34	7,973	0.734
Iran	72.0	10,850	43	16,673	0.782
Iraq	30.7	–	–	–	–
Ireland	4.4	35,710	34	91,432	0.965
Israel	7.3	27,450	39	64,633	0.935
Italy	59.8	30,800	36	120,897	0.951
Jamaica	2.7	7,370	46	9,601	0.766
Japan	127.7	35,190	–	124,858	0.960
Jordan	5.9	5,720	39	10,792	0.770
Kazakhstan	15.7	9,720	34	13,723	0.804
Kenya	38.8	1,560	43	3,442	0.541
Kiribati	0.1	3,620	–	–	–
Korea, North	23.8	–	–	–	–
Korea, South	48.6	27,840	32	45,278	0.937
Kuwait	2.7	53,480	–	–	0.916
Kyrgyzstan	5.3	2,150	30	5,174	0.710
Laos	6.2	2,050	35	–	0.619
Latvia	2.3	16,010	38	18,958	0.866

Food expenditure as % of household expenditure on consumables *latest available 1998–2008*	Military expenditure as % of spending on healthcare and education *2007–08*	National minimum wage as % of GDP per capita *2008–09*	Healthcare % of total healthcare that is privately funded *2006*	Child labor % of 5–14 year olds working disproportionate hours *1999–2007*	
–	30%	–	25%	8%	Djibouti
–	–	76%	37%	–	Dominica
–	14%	18%	62%	10%	Dominican Republic
30%	–	218%	13%	4%	East Timor
31%	88%	74%	56%	12%	Ecuador
–	40%	–	57%	7%	Egypt
–	8%	28%	38%	6%	El Salvador
–	–	–	19%	28%	Equatorial Guinea
–	571%	95%	53%	–	Eritrea
31%	25%	28%	26%	–	Estonia
51%	22%	127%	39%	53%	Ethiopia
29%	16%	–	30%	–	Fiji
21%	10%	–	23%	–	Finland
21%	16%	51%	20%	–	France
–	15%	21%	26%	–	Gabon
–	14%	118%	43%	25%	Gambia
64%	195%	6%	76%	18%	Georgia
19%	–	–	23%	–	Germany
–	11%	53%	63%	34%	Ghana
38%	33%	44%	37%	–	Greece
–	–	61%	36%	–	Grenada
37%	8%	58%	62%	29%	Guatemala
–	87%	–	81%	25%	Guinea
–	–	194%	70%	39%	Guinea–Bissau
–	–	67%	14%	19%	Guyana
58%	–	60%	32%	21%	Haiti
–	–	189%	52%	16%	Honduras
29%	12%	31%	28%	–	Hungary
15%	–	–	17%	–	Iceland
50%	61%	–	74%	12%	India
48%	25%	28%	49%	4%	Indonesia
–	35%	59%	47%	–	Iran
–	–	38%	22%	11%	Iraq
26%	5%	42%	20%	–	Ireland
–	81%	45%	43%	–	Israel
22%	15%	–	22%	–	Italy
55%	8%	50%	45%	6%	Jamaica
20%	9%	32%	18%	–	Japan
36%	–	54%	56%	–	Jordan
45%	25%	12%	35%	2%	Kazakhstan
46%	19%	51%	52%	26%	Kenya
–	–	188%	12%	4%	Kiribati
–	–	–	14%	–	Korea, North
23%	33%	37%	44%	–	Korea, South
–	71%	21%	22%	–	Kuwait
–	33%	12%	57%	–	Kyrgyzstan
52%	13%	48%	79%	25%	Laos
34%	20%	27%	39%	–	Latvia

Income, Expenditure, & Earnings

	Total population millions 2008	GNI per capita PPP$ 2008 or latest available	Gini index latest available 1995–2004	Wealth per household PPP$ 2000	Human Development Index score 2007
Lebanon	4.2	11,750	–	20,560	0.803
Lesotho	2.0	1,970	63	2,876	0.514
Liberia	3.8	310	–	–	0.442
Libya	6.3	16,270	–	–	0.847
Lithuania	3.4	17,170	36	21,566	0.870
Luxembourg	0.5	52,770	–	185,231	0.960
Macedonia	2.0	9,250	39	14,759	0.817
Madagascar	19.1	1,050	48	2,226	0.543
Malawi	14.8	810	39	2,559	0.493
Malaysia	27.0	13,740	49	12,458	0.829
Maldives	0.3	5,290	–	–	0.771
Mali	12.7	1,100	40	1,798	0.371
Malta	0.4	20,580	–	74,246	0.902
Marshall Islands	0.1	–	–	–	–
Mauritania	3.2	1,990	39	3,966	0.520
Mauritius	1.3	12,580	–	60,398	0.804
Mexico	106.4	14,340	46	23,488	0.854
Micronesia, Fed. States	0.1	3,270	–	–	–
Moldova	3.6	3,270	33	7,790	0.720
Mongolia	2.6	3,470	33	–	0.727
Montenegro	0.6	13,420	–	–	0.834
Morocco	31.6	4,190	40	12,440	0.654
Mozambique	22.4	770	47	2,820	0.402
Namibia	2.1	6,250	–	8,843	0.686
Nauru	0.01	–	–	–	–
Nepal	28.8	1,120	47	–	0.553
Netherlands	16.4	40,620	31	121,165	0.964
New Zealand	4.3	25,200	36	55,823	0.950
Nicaragua	5.7	2,620	43	5,161	0.699
Niger	14.7	680	51	1,755	0.340
Nigeria	151.2	1,980	44	905	0.511
Niue	0.05	–	–	–	–
Norway	4.8	59,250	26	79,292	0.971
Oman	2.8	22,170	–	–	0.846
Pakistan	166.1	2,590	31	5,987	0.572
Palau	0.02	–	–	–	–
Palestinian Territories	3.9	–	–	–	0.737
Panama	3.4	12,630	56	15,003	0.840
Papua New Guinea	6.6	2,030	51	3,629	0.541
Paraguay	6.2	4,660	58	10,879	0.761
Peru	28.8	7,950	52	11,577	0.806
Philippines	90.3	3,900	45	12,453	0.751
Poland	38.1	16,710	35	24,654	0.880
Portugal	10.6	22,330	39	53,811	0.909
Puerto Rico	4.0	–	–	77,876	–
Qatar	1.3	–	–	14,806	0.910
Romania	21.5	13,380	31	–	0.837
Russia	142.0	15,460	40	16,579	0.817

Food expenditure as % of household expenditure on consumables *latest available 1998–2008*	Military expenditure as % of spending on healthcare and education *2007–08*	National minimum wage as % of GDP per capita *2008–09*	Healthcare % of total healthcare that is privately funded *2006*	Child labor % of 5–14 year olds working disproportionate hours *1999–2007*	
–	86%	52%	55%	7%	Lebanon
44%	15%	56%	41%	23%	Lesotho
–	13%	–	74%	–	Liberia
–	–	8%	33%	–	Libya
41%	17%	29%	30%	–	Lithuania
19%	–	25%	9%	–	Luxembourg
50%	23%	–	29%	6%	Macedonia
–	22%	108%	37%	32%	Madagascar
66%	12%	62%	30%	29%	Malawi
37%	32%	31%	55%	–	Malaysia
30%	–	67%	20%	–	Maldives
–	31%	117%	50%	34%	Mali
–	6%	58%	22%	–	Malta
–	–	–	91%	–	Marshall Islands
–	50%	98%	30%	4%	Mauritania
38%	3%	15%	47%	–	Mauritius
34%	5%	11%	55%	16%	Mexico
–	–	118%	1%	–	Micronesia, Fed. States
51%	4%	26%	52%	32%	Moldova
–	18%	56%	26%	18%	Mongolia
–	–	16%	28%	10%	Montenegro
–	46%	64%	70%	11%	Morocco
55%	11%	–	29%	–	Mozambique
24%	29%	–	33%	13%	Namibia
–	–	–	32%	–	Nauru
59%	39%	186%	68%	31%	Nepal
13%	12%	47%	19%	–	Netherlands
19%	8%	62%	22%	–	New Zealand
48%	9%	84%	51%	15%	Nicaragua
30%	13%	193%	45%	43%	Niger
–	–	66%	68%	13%	Nigeria
–	–	–	87%	–	Niue
17%	11%	–	15%	–	Norway
–	181%	23%	16%	–	Oman
48%	96%	110%	81%	–	Pakistan
–	–	64%	19%	–	Palau
33%	–	–	–	–	Palestinian Territories
26%	–	37%	31%	3%	Panama
–	–	54%	18%	–	Papua New Guinea
–	12%	142%	59%	15%	Paraguay
32%	24%	51%	41%	19%	Peru
46%	24%	59%	66%	12%	Philippines
32%	20%	46%	30%	–	Poland
29%	16%	42%	29%	3%	Portugal
–	–	–	–	–	Puerto Rico
–	–	–	22%	–	Qatar
49%	23%	28%	23%	1%	Romania
–	48%	18%	37%	–	Russia

Income, Expenditure, & Earnings

	Total population millions 2008	GNI per capita PPP$ 2008 or latest available	Gini index latest available 1995–2004	Wealth per household PPP$ 2000	Human Development Index score 2007
Rwanda	9.7	1,110	47	2,955	0.460
Saint Kitts & Nevis	0.05	15,490	–	22,339	0.838
Saint Lucia	0.2	9,020	–	18,013	0.821
Saint Vincent & Grenadines	0.1	8,570	–	13,287	0.772
Samoa	0.2	4,410	–	–	0.771
São Tomé & Principe	0.2	1,790	–	3,235	0.651
Saudi Arabia	24.6	24,500	–	22,025	0.843
Senegal	12.2	1,780	41	4,309	0.464
Serbia	7.4	10,380	–	–	0.826
Seychelles	0.1	19,650	–	26,484	0.845
Sierra Leone	5.6	770	–	2,043	0.365
Singapore	4.8	47,970	43	113,632	0.944
Slovakia	5.4	21,460	26	24,049	0.880
Slovenia	2.0	27,160	28	37,019	0.929
Solomon Islands	0.5	2,230	–	–	0.610
Somalia	8.9	–	–	–	–
South Africa	48.7	9,790	58	16,266	0.683
Spain	45.6	30,830	35	93,086	0.955
Sri Lanka	20.2	4,460	40	10,337	0.759
Sudan	41.3	1,920	–	–	0.531
Suriname	0.5	6,680	–	–	0.769
Swaziland	1.2	5,000	50	12,773	0.572
Sweden	9.2	37,780	25	78,148	0.963
Switzerland	7.6	39,210	34	137,549	0.960
Syria	20.6	4,490	–	8,917	0.742
Tajikistan	6.8	1,870	33	2,940	0.688
Tanzania	42.5	1,260	35	1,216	0.530
Thailand	67.4	7,770	42	13,920	0.783
Togo	6.5	830	–	2,217	0.499
Tonga	0.1	3,980	–	–	0.768
Trinidad & Tobago	1.3	24,240	–	51,101	0.837
Tunisia	10.3	7,460	40	20,534	0.769
Turkey	73.9	13,420	44	22,379	0.806
Turkmenistan	5.0	6,130	41	–	0.739
Tuvalu	0.01	–	–	–	–
Uganda	31.7	1,140	46	2,889	0.514
Ukraine	46.3	7,210	28	9,547	0.796
United Arab Emirates	4.5	45,660	–	–	0.903
United Kingdom	61.4	36,240	36	128,959	0.947
United States of America	304.1	46,790	41	143,727	0.956
Uruguay	3.3	12,550	45	20,926	0.865
Uzbekistan	27.3	2,660	37	–	0.710
Vanuatu	0.2	3,480	–	–	0.693
Venezuela	27.9	12,850	48	14,711	0.844
Vietnam	86.2	2,700	34	5,621	0.725
Yemen	22.9	2,220	33	1,426	0.575
Zambia	12.6	1,230	51	2,010	0.481
Zimbabwe	12.5	170	50	6,104	–

Food expenditure as % of household expenditure on consumables *latest available 1998–2008*	Military expenditure as % of spending on healthcare and education *2007–08*	National minimum wage as % of GDP per capita *2008–09*	Healthcare % of total healthcare that is privately funded *2006*	Child labor % of 5–14 year olds working disproportionate hours *1999–2007*	
72%	20%	51%	57%	35%	Rwanda
–	–	59%	38%	–	Saint Kitts & Nevis
–	–	12%	41%	–	Saint Lucia
–	–	43%	37%	–	Saint Vincent & Grenadines
–	–	59%	15%	–	Samoa
–	–	49%	15%	8%	São Tomé & Principe
–	100%	25%	23%	–	Saudi Arabia
53%	20%	91%	43%	22%	Senegal
45%	–	43%	30%	4%	Serbia
37%	23%	29%	24%	–	Seychelles
49%	36%	30%	63%	48%	Sierra Leone
22%	95%	–	64%	–	Singapore
22%	17%	28%	29%	–	Slovakia
26%	13%	38%	28%	–	Slovenia
–	–	50%	8%	–	Solomon Islands
–	–	–	–	49%	Somalia
25%	18%	25%	62%	–	South Africa
22%	12%	36%	28%	–	Spain
40%	–	37%	52%	8%	Sri Lanka
–	–	47%	63%	13%	Sudan
–	–	47%	57%	–	Suriname
–	16%	16%	34%	9%	Swaziland
17%	10%	–	18%	–	Sweden
24%	7%	36%	41%	–	Switzerland
–	66%	57%	52%	4%	Syria
70%	48%	26%	75%	10%	Tajikistan
65%	–	125%	42%	36%	Tanzania
39%	21%	28%	34%	8%	Thailand
64%	30%	173%	79%	29%	Togo
44%	17%	–	25%	–	Tonga
–	–	16%	43%	1%	Trinidad & Tobago
–	14%	38%	56%	–	Tunisia
35%	32%	56%	27%	5%	Turkey
–	–	44%	33%	–	Turkmenistan
–	–	175%	3%	–	Tuvalu
44%	44%	9%	74%	36%	Uganda
61%	32%	35%	44%	7%	Ukraine
–	62%	–	30%	–	United Arab Emirates
23%	19%	61%	9%	–	United Kingdom
14%	31%	32%	54%	–	United States of America
–	20%	24%	56%	8%	Uruguay
35%	–	22%	50%	2%	Uzbekistan
–	–	126%	34%	–	Vanuatu
–	21%	47%	50%	8%	Venezuela
51%	28%	38%	67%	16%	Vietnam
–	70%	–	53%	11%	Yemen
64%	25%	75%	38%	12%	Zambia
–	21%	–	51%	13%	Zimbabwe

Access to Health & Services

	Life expectancy Average years at birth 2009	Maternal mortality per 100,000 live births 2005	Child mortality per 1,000 live births 2005	Under nourished as % of population 2004–06	Piped water % of rural households with 2006	Diarrheal disease DALYS lost per 1,000 people 2002
Afghanistan	44.4	1,800	257	–	0%	52.0
Albania	78.0	92	15	–	72%	0.3
Algeria	74.0	180	37	–	55%	8.0
Angola	38.5	1,400	158	44%	1%	109.0
Antigua & Barbuda	74.8	–	11	27%	–	1.1
Argentina	76.6	77	16	–	45%	1.1
Armenia	72.7	76	24	23%	74%	1.0
Australia	81.6	4	6	–	–	0.2
Austria	79.5	4	4	–	100%	0.1
Azerbaijan	66.7	82	39	11%	19%	3.9
Bahamas	69.9	16	13	6%	–	1.1
Bahrain	75.2	32	10	–	–	–
Bangladesh	60.3	570	61	26%	0%	14.0
Barbados	73.9	16	12	–	–	0.6
Belarus	70.6	18	13	–	68%	0.3
Belgium	79.2	8	5	–	–	0.2
Belize	68.2	52	25	–	–	4.4
Benin	59.0	840	123	19%	2%	33.0
Bhutan	66.1	440	84	–	9%	18.0
Bolivia	66.9	290	57	23%	45%	15.0
Bosnia & Herzegovina	78.5	3	14	–	72%	0.3
Botswana	61.9	380	40	26%	28%	6.6
Brazil	72.0	110	22	6%	17%	3.6
Brunei	75.7	13	9	–	–	–
Bulgaria	73.1	11	12	–	–	0.2
Burkina Faso	53.0	700	191	9%	0%	51.0
Burma	63.4	380	103	17%	2%	15.0
Burundi	57.8	1,100	180	63%	1%	41.0
Cambodia	62.1	540	91	25%	5%	25.0
Cameroon	53.7	1,000	148	23%	2%	27.0
Canada	81.2	7	6	–	38%	0.2
Cape Verde	71.6	210	32	14%	–	7.0
Central African Republic	44.5	980	172	41%	0%	35.0
Chad	47.7	1,500	209	38%	1%	40.0
Chile	77.3	16	9	–	46%	1.0
China	73.5	45	22	10%	62%	3.0
Colombia	74.1	130	20	10%	63%	3.0
Comoros	63.5	400	66	51%	3%	16.0
Congo	54.2	740	125	21%	3%	13.0
Congo, Dem. Rep.	54.4	1,100	161	75%	1%	64.0
Cook Islands	74.2	–	18	–	–	2.0
Costa Rica	77.6	30	11	–	95%	1.0
Côte d'Ivoire	55.5	810	127	14%	13%	29.0
Croatia	75.4	7	6	–	71%	0.2
Cuba	77.5	45	7	–	49%	1.0
Cyprus	77.5	10	5	–	100%	0.5
Czech Republic	76.8	4	4	–	91%	0.1
Denmark	78.3	3	4	–	100%	0.2

Energy consumption kg of oil equivalent per capita 2007	CO_2 emissions tonnes per capita per year 2008	Modern fuels % lacking access 2007	Mobility % of rural population within 2 km of all-season road	Literacy % of population with basic skills latest 1999–2007	Primary education % of children enrolled 2007	
–	0.0	88%	22%	28%	–	Afghanistan
694	1.3	–	31%	99%	–	Albania
1,089	3.1	1%	59%	75%	95%	Algeria
606	1.9	48%	42%	67%	–	Angola
–	8.1	3%	–	99%	74%	Antigua & Barbuda
1,850	4.3	5%	77%	98%	98%	Argentina
926	3.7	–	80%	100%	85%	Armenia
5,888	20.8	–	–	99%	97%	Australia
3,997	8.6	–	95%	99%	97%	Austria
1,388	4.7	–	67%	100%	95%	Azerbaijan
–	17.5	5%	82%	96%	91%	Bahamas
11,551	43.2	5%	99%	89%	98%	Bahrain
163	0.3	91%	37%	54%	87%	Bangladesh
–	5.1	5%	100%	100%	97%	Barbados
2,891	7.0	–	64%	100%	90%	Belarus
5,366	14.9	–	100%	99%	98%	Belgium
–	3.3	16%	78%	75%	97%	Belize
343	0.4	94%	32%	41%	80%	Benin
–	0.5	43%	47%	53%	87%	Bhutan
571	1.4	31%	48%	91%	94%	Bolivia
1,483	4.1	–	81%	97%	–	Bosnia & Herzegovina
1,068	2.4	44%	79%	83%	84%	Botswana
1,239	2.2	13%	53%	90%	93%	Brazil
7,190	27.3	–	81%	–	93%	Brunei
2,641	7.3	–	98%	98%	95%	Bulgaria
–	0.1	93%	25%	29%	58%	Burkina Faso
319	0.3	97%	23%	–	–	Burma
–	0.0	100%	19%	59%	81%	Burundi
358	0.3	93%	81%	76%	89%	Cambodia
391	0.4	79%	20%	68%	85%	Cameroon
8,169	17.3	–	–	99%	–	Canada
–	0.7	38%	82%	84%	–	Cape Verde
–	0.1	99%	–	49%	56%	Central African Republic
–	0.0	98%	5%	32%	–	Chad
1,851	3.9	5%	76%	97%	94%	Chile
1,484	4.9	58%	97%	93%	–	China
655	1.5	18%	78%	93%	87%	Colombia
–	0.2	76%	73%	75%	–	Comoros
357	1.4	83%	48%	81%	54%	Congo
289	0.0	95%	26%	67%	–	Congo, Dem. Rep.
–	7.4	6%	–	–	67%	Cook Islands
1,070	1.7	14%	82%	96%	90%	Costa Rica
496	0.3	86%	56%	49%	–	Côte d'Ivoire
2,101	5.4	–	84%	99%	–	Croatia
884	2.3	–	81%	100%	98%	Cuba
2,854	9.5	5%	89%	98%	99%	Cyprus
4,428	9.9	–	97%	99%	93%	Czech Republic
3,598	9.9	–	99%	99%	96%	Denmark

Access to Health & Services

	Life expectancy Average years at birth 2009	Maternal mortality per 100,000 live births 2005	Child mortality per 1,000 live births 2005	Under nourished as % of population 2004–06	Piped water % of rural households with 2006	Diarrheal disease DALYS lost per 1,000 people 2002
Djibouti	60.3	650	127	31%	8%	35.0
Dominica	75.6	–	11	–	–	1.0
Dominican Republic	73.7	150	38	21%	62%	5.0
East Timor	67.3	380	97	23%	11%	6.0
Ecuador	75.3	210	22	13%	65%	5.0
Egypt	72.1	130	36	–	82%	6.0
El Salvador	72.3	170	24	10%	38%	5.0
Equatorial Guinea	61.6	680	206	–	0%	27.0
Eritrea	61.8	450	70	66%	0%	20.0
Estonia	72.8	25	6	–	75%	0.2
Ethiopia	55.4	720	119	44%	1%	28.0
Fiji	70.7	210	18	–	7%	2.0
Finland	79.0	7	4	–	–	0.2
France	81.0	8	4	–	100%	–
Gabon	53.1	520	91	–	8%	10.0
Gambia	53.8	690	109	29%	5%	19.0
Georgia	76.7	66	30	12%	38%	0.3
Germany	79.3	4	4	–	97%	0.1
Ghana	60.1	560	115	8%	4%	14.0
Greece	79.7	3	4	–	99%	–
Grenada	66.0	–	19	23%	–	2.0
Guatemala	70.3	290	39	16%	67%	9.0
Guinea	57.1	910	150	16%	1%	33.0
Guinea–Bissau	47.9	1,100	198	31%	1%	33.0
Guyana	66.3	470	60	6%	61%	10.0
Haiti	60.8	670	76	58%	4%	20.0
Honduras	70.5	280	24	12%	67%	8.0
Hungary	73.4	6	7	–	93%	0.2
Iceland	80.7	4	3	–	100%	0.2
India	66.1	450	72	22%	10%	13.0
Indonesia	70.8	420	31	16%	7%	5.0
Iran	71.1	140	33	–	–	–
Iraq	70.0	300	44	–	48%	17.0
Ireland	78.2	1	4	–	96%	–
Israel	80.7	4	5	–	98%	–
Italy	80.2	3	4	–	96%	–
Jamaica	73.5	170	31	5%	47%	2.0
Japan	82.1	6	4	–	94%	0.2
Jordan	79.9	62	24	–	81%	4.0
Kazakhstan	67.9	140	32	–	24%	1.0
Kenya	57.9	560	121	30%	12%	23.0
Kiribati	63.2	–	63	5%	22%	10.0
Korea, North	63.8	370	55	32%	71%	5.0
Korea, South	78.7	14	5	–	–	–
Kuwait	77.7	4	11	–	–	–
Kyrgyzstan	69.4	150	38	–	33%	5.0
Laos	56.6	660	70	19%	8%	28.0
Latvia	72.2	10	9	–	59%	0.3

Energy consumption kg of oil equivalent per capita 2007	CO$_2$ emissions tonnes per capita per year 2008	Modern fuels % lacking access 2007	Mobility % of rural population within 2 km of all-season road	Literacy % of population with basic skills latest 1999–2007	Primary education % of children enrolled 2007	
–	2.6	14%	81%	70%	45%	Djibouti
–	1.7	–	88%	88%	–	Dominica
804	2.0	12%	62%	89%	82%	Dominican Republic
–	0.3	–	90%	–	63%	East Timor
885	2.0	9%	73%	91%	97%	Ecuador
840	2.1	0%	77%	66%	96%	Egypt
800	0.9	26%	64%	82%	92%	El Salvador
–	7.4	–	53%	87%	67%	Equatorial Guinea
151	0.1	67%	29%	64%	41%	Eritrea
4,198	15.8	–	86%	100%	95%	Estonia
290	0.1	96%	32%	36%	71%	Ethiopia
–	2.9	48%	76%	94%	91%	Fiji
6,895	10.4	–	82%	99%	96%	Finland
4,258	6.5	–	99%	99%	99%	France
1,300	3.1	32%	45%	86%	–	Gabon
–	0.2	95%	77%	43%	67%	Gambia
767	1.2	–	82%	100%	94%	Georgia
4,027	10.1	–	89%	99%	98%	Germany
415	0.3	89%	61%	65%	73%	Ghana
2,875	10.0	–	90%	97%	100%	Greece
–	3.7	–	98%	96%	76%	Grenada
620	0.9	63%	55%	73%	95%	Guatemala
–	0.1	100%	22%	30%	74%	Guinea
–	0.3	99%	52%	65%	–	Guinea–Bissau
–	2.2	11%	46%	99%	–	Guyana
286	0.2	94%	–	62%	–	Haiti
661	1.1	55%	40%	84%	93%	Honduras
2,658	5.7	–	98%	99%	87%	Hungary
15,708	11.1	–	81%	99%	97%	Iceland
529	1.3	71%	61%	66%	89%	India
849	1.8	54%	94%	92%	95%	Indonesia
2,604	7.8	–	66%	82%	94%	Iran
1,105	3.6	5%	58%	74%	89%	Iraq
3,457	10.7	–	93%	99%	96%	Ireland
3,059	9.9	–	88%	97%	97%	Israel
3,001	7.8	–	98%	99%	99%	Italy
1,852	4.7	18%	93%	86%	86%	Jamaica
4,019	9.5	–	99%	99%	100%	Japan
1,259	3.6	0%	79%	91%	89%	Jordan
4,292	13.0	–	77%	100%	90%	Kazakhstan
485	0.3	83%	44%	74%	86%	Kenya
–	0.4	–	–	–	–	Kiribati
774	3.1	–	44%	–	–	Korea, North
4,586	11.2	0%	89%	99%	98%	Korea, South
9,463	31.6	5%	82%	95%	88%	Kuwait
556	1.1	–	76%	99%	84%	Kyrgyzstan
–	0.2	97%	64%	–	86%	Laos
2,052	4.4	–	90%	100%	90%	Latvia

Access to Health & Services

	Life expectancy Average years at birth 2009	Maternal mortality per 100,000 live births 2005	Child mortality per 1,000 live births 2005	Under nourished as % of population 2004–06	Piped water % of rural households with 2006	Diarrheal disease DALYS lost per 1,000 people 2002
Lebanon	73.7	150	29	–	–	2.0
Lesotho	40.4	960	84	15%	5%	24.0
Liberia	41.8	1,200	133	38%	0%	44.0
Libya	77.3	97	18	–	–	–
Lithuania	74.9	11	8	–	–	–
Luxembourg	79.3	12	3	–	98%	0.2
Macedonia	74.7	10	17	–	84%	–
Madagascar	62.9	510	112	35%	2%	33.0
Malawi	50.0	1,100	111	29%	2%	47.0
Malaysia	73.3	62	11	–	87%	1.0
Maldives	74.0	120	30	7%	0%	5.0
Mali	51.8	970	196	10%	2%	53.0
Malta	79.4	8	5	–	94%	–
Marshall Islands	71.2	–	54	–	–	6.0
Mauritania	60.4	820	119	8%	14%	38.0
Mauritius	74.0	15	15	6%	100%	1.0
Mexico	76.1	60	35	–	73%	2.0
Micronesia, Fed. States	70.9	–	40	–	–	10.0
Moldova	70.8	22	18	–	12%	0.4
Mongolia	67.7	46	43	29%	6%	11.0
Montenegro	–	14	10	–	66%	0.6
Morocco	75.5	240	34	–	15%	7.0
Mozambique	41.2	520	168	37%	2%	47.0
Namibia	51.2	210	68	19%	28%	13.0
Nauru	64.2	–	30	–	–	–
Nepal	65.5	830	55	16%	11%	20.0
Netherlands	79.4	6	5	–	100%	0.2
New Zealand	80.4	9	6	–	–	–
Nicaragua	71.5	170	35	21%	27%	8.0
Niger	52.6	1,800	176	28%	–	65.0
Nigeria	46.9	1,100	189	8%	2%	32.0
Niue	–	–	–	–	–	0.5
Norway	80.0	7	4	–	100%	0.2
Oman	74.2	64	12	–	–	–
Pakistan	65.3	320	90	23%	19%	22.0
Palau	71.2	–	10	–	–	2.0
Palestinian Territories	74.5	–	27	15%	64%	–
Panama	77.3	130	23	17%	79%	3.0
Papua New Guinea	65.8	470	65	–	4%	13.0
Paraguay	75.8	150	29	12%	29%	5.0
Peru	70.7	240	20	13%	44%	6.0
Philippines	71.1	230	28	15%	24%	5.0
Poland	75.6	8	7	–	96%	–
Portugal	78.2	11	4	–	99%	–
Puerto Rico	78.5	18	–	–	–	–
Qatar	75.4	12	15	–	–	0.6
Romania	72.5	24	15	–	8%	–
Russia	66.0	28	15	–	52%	0.3

Energy consumption kg of oil equivalent per capita 2007	CO$_2$ emissions tonnes per capita per year 2008	Modern fuels % lacking access 2007	Mobility % of rural population within 2 km of all-season road	Literacy % of population with basic skills latest 1999–2007	Primary education % of children enrolled 2007	
959	3.6	0%	87%	90%	83%	Lebanon
–	0.1	63%	67%	82%	72%	Lesotho
–	0.2	100%	66%	56%	31%	Liberia
2,889	9.3	5%	78%	–	–	Libya
2,740	5.1	–	97%	100%	90%	Lithuania
8,790	23.9	–	–	99%	97%	Luxembourg
1,482	3.6	–	78%	97%	89%	Macedonia
–	0.1	99%	25%	71%	98%	Madagascar
–	0.1	99%	38%	72%	87%	Malawi
2,733	6.4	3%	82%	92%	97%	Malaysia
–	2.3	19%	–	97%	96%	Maldives
–	0.1	100%	14%	26%	63%	Mali
2,120	7.9	34%	100%	92%	91%	Malta
–	–	–	–	–	66%	Marshall Islands
–	0.9	63%	31%	56%	80%	Mauritania
–	3.6	4%	70%	87%	95%	Mauritius
1,750	4.0	14%	61%	93%	98%	Mexico
–	–	42%	82%	–	–	Micronesia, Fed. States.
910	1.7	–	66%	99%	88%	Moldova
1,182	2.4	77%	36%	97%	89%	Mongolia
–	5.5	–	74%	96%	–	Montenegro
460	1.3	9%	36%	56%	89%	Morocco
418	0.1	97%	27%	44%	76%	Mozambique
745	1.5	65%	57%	88%	87%	Namibia
–	14.7	9%	–	–	72%	Nauru
338	0.1	84%	17%	57%	80%	Nepal
4,909	15.9	–	100%	99%	98%	Netherlands
3,966	9.4	–	83%	99%	99%	New Zealand
621	0.9	58%	28%	78%	96%	Nicaragua
–	0.1	99%	37%	29%	45%	Niger
722	0.7	76%	47%	72%	64%	Nigeria
–	NA	12%	–	–	–	Niue
5,704	8.7	–	83%	99%	99%	Norway
5,678	13.2	5%	81%	84%	73%	Oman
512	0.9	68%	61%	54%	66%	Pakistan
–	–	1%	–	92%	–	Palau
–	0.8	1%	–	–	73%	Palestinian Territories
845	4.6	19%	77%	93%	98%	Panama
–	0.8	87%	68%	58%	–	Papua New Guinea
686	0.6	49%	54%	95%	94%	Paraguay
494	1.2	39%	43%	90%	96%	Peru
451	0.8	51%	80%	93%	91%	Philippines
2,547	7.8	–	95%	99%	96%	Poland
2,363	5.4	–	88%	95%	99%	Portugal
–	8.0	–	98%	–	–	Puerto Rico
19,504	74.1	0%	81%	93%	93%	Qatar
1,806	4.6	–	89%	98%	94%	Romania
4,730	12.3	–	81%	–	–	Russia

Access to Health & Services

	Life expectancy Average years at birth 2009	Maternal mortality per 100,000 live births 2005	Child mortality per 1,000 live births 2005	Under nourished as % of population 2004–06	Piped water % of rural households with 2006	Diarrheal disease DALYS lost per 1,000 people 2002
Rwanda	56.8	1,300	181	40%	1%	47.0
Saint Kitts &Nevis	73.2	–	18	15%	–	2.0
Saint Lucia	76.5	–	18	8%	–	1.7
Saint Vincent & Grenadines	73.7	–	19	6%	–	–
Samoa	71.9	–	27	–	–	3.3
São Tomé & Principe	68.3	–	99	5%	17%	11.0
Saudi Arabia	76.3	18	25	–	–	–
Senegal	59.0	980	114	25%	18%	22.0
Serbia	73.9	14	8	–	–	0.6
Seychelles	73.0	–	13	8%	–	–
Sierra Leone	55.3	2,100	262	46%	1%	78.0
Singapore	82.0	14	3	–	–	0.4
Slovakia	75.4	6	8	–	94%	0.2
Slovenia	76.9	6	4	–	–	–
Solomon Islands	73.7	220	70	9%	1%	14.0
Somalia	49.6	1,400	142	–	0%	48.0
South Africa	49.0	400	59	–	42%	9.0
Spain	80.1	4	4	–	100%	0.2
Sri Lanka	75.1	58	21	21%	3%	1.5
Sudan	51.4	450	109	20%	13%	18.0
Suriname	73.7	72	29	7%	46%	4.0
Swaziland	47.9	390	91	18%	15%	17.0
Sweden	80.9	3	3	–	100%	0.1
Switzerland	80.9	5	5	–	99%	0.1
Syria	74.2	130	17	–	68%	4.0
Tajikistan	65.3	170	67	26%	23%	10.0
Tanzania	52.0	950	116	35%	4%	26.0
Thailand	73.1	110	7	17%	35%	2.0
Togo	59.7	510	100	37%	0%	18.0
Tonga	70.7	–	23	–	–	3.0
Trinidad & Tobago	70.9	45	35	10%	72%	1.0
Tunisia	75.8	100	21	–	39%	2.0
Turkey	72.0	44	23	–	86%	3.0
Turkmenistan	67.9	130	50	6%	–	7.0
Tuvalu	69.3	–	37	–	–	8.0
Uganda	52.7	550	130	15%	1%	35.0
Ukraine	68.3	18	24	–	51%	0.3
United Arab Emirates	76.1	37	8	–	70%	0.6
United Kingdom	79.0	8	6	–	98%	–
United States of America	78.1	11	8	–	46%	0.2
Uruguay	76.4	20	14	–	84%	1.0
Uzbekistan	72.0	24	41	13%	28%	1.0
Vanuatu	64.0	–	34	6%	–	5.0
Venezuela	73.6	57	19	12%	–	3.0
Vietnam	71.7	150	15	13%	8%	4.0
Yemen	63.0	430	73	32%	6%	29.0
Zambia	38.6	830	170	45%	2%	42.0
Zimbabwe	45.8	880	90	39%	6%	14.0

Energy consumption kg of oil equivalent per capita 2007	CO$_2$ emissions tonnes per capita per year 2008	Modern fuels % lacking access 2007	Mobility % of rural population within 2 km of all-season road	Literacy % of population with basic skills latest 1999–2007	Primary education % of children enrolled 2007	
–	0.1	100%	52%	65%	94%	Rwanda
–	4.9	5%	89%	98%	87%	Saint Kitts & Nevis
–	2.6	14%	89%	95%	98%	Saint Lucia
–	2.1	–	97%	88%	91%	Saint Vincent & Grenadines
–	0.8	81%	71%	99%	–	Samoa
–	0.6	–	83%	88%	97%	São Tomé & Principe
6,223	16.6	5%	75%	85%	85%	Saudi Arabia
225	0.5	59%	29%	42%	72%	Senegal
2,141	5.5	–	74%	96%	95%	Serbia
–	12.5	5%	–	92%	–	Seychelles
–	0.2	93%	65%	38%	–	Sierra Leone
5,831	34.6	100%	–	94%	–	Singapore
3,307	6.9	–	–	99%	92%	Slovakia
3,632	8.3	–	95%	100%	96%	Slovenia
–	0.4	17%	77%	77%	62%	Solomon Islands
–	0.1	81%	40%	–	–	Somalia
2,807	9.2	17%	21%	88%	86%	South Africa
3,208	8.9	–	95%	98%	100%	Spain
464	0.6	81%	92%	91%	–	Sri Lanka
363	0.3	93%	5%	61%	–	Sudan
–	4.5	–	79%	90%	94%	Suriname
–	0.8	76%	86%	80%	87%	Swaziland
5,512	6.2	–	–	99%	94%	Sweden
3,406	6.1	–	–	99%	89%	Switzerland
978	2.5	1%	49%	–	–	Syria
580	0.9	–	74%	100%	97%	Tajikistan
443	0.1	97%	38%	72%	98%	Tanzania
1,553	3.9	37%	33%	94%	95%	Thailand
390	0.5	98%	22%	53%	77%	Togo
–	1.7	41%	86%	99%	96%	Tonga
11,506	41.0	1%	91%	99%	94%	Trinidad & Tobago
864	2.1	2%	39%	78%	95%	Tunisia
1,370	3.6	–	69%	89%	92%	Turkey
3,631	11.8	–	66%	100%	–	Turkmenistan
–	–	29%	–	–	–	Tuvalu
–	0.1	100%	27%	74%	95%	Uganda
2,953	7.6	–	56%	100%	89%	Ukraine
11,832	43.1	1%	76%	90%	91%	United Arab Emirates
3,464	9.4	–	96%	99%	97%	United Kingdom
7,766	19.2	–	86%	99%	92%	United States of America
953	2.2	4%	84%	98%	97%	Uruguay
1,812	4.6	–	57%	97%	91%	Uzbekistan
–	0.5	86%	77%	78%	87%	Vanuatu
2,319	7.0	–	78%	–	92%	Venezuela
655	1.1	66%	84%	90%	–	Vietnam
324	0.9	37%	21%	59%	75%	Yemen
604	0.3	84%	64%	71%	94%	Zambia
759	1.0	67%	65%	–	88%	Zimbabwe

Glossary

Agriculture: The provision of goods and food through farming.

Child labor: For children aged 5–11 years: at least one hour of economic activity or at least 28 hours of domestic work a week. For children aged 12–14 years old: at least 14 hours of economic activity or at least 28 hours of domestic work a week.

Communicable disease: One that can be communicated from one person to another.

Corruption Perceptions Index: A measure of the level of public-sector corruption, based on 13 different expert and business surveys that ask questions relating to the abuse of public power for private benefit.

Decile: One of 10 equal parts (a tenth, or 10% of a whole).

Democracy Index: The Economist Intelligence Unit's democracy index is based on five categories: electoral process and pluralism; civil liberties; the functioning of government; political participation; and political culture.

Developing countries: Poor, or non-industrialized, countries.

Disability Adjusted Life Year (DALY): The equivalent of one year of healthy life lost due to illness and disability.

Gender Empowerment Measure: An evaluation of the extent to which women are able to actively participate in economic and political life, and to take part in decision-making.

Gini index: A measure of inequality based on the Gini coefficient, which compares actual distribution to an equal distribution. In the representation in this atlas, a value of 100 = absolute inequality. A value of 0 = absolute equality.

GDP/GNP/GNI: Measures of the annual output of goods and services from a country or region. *Gross Domestic Product* includes all production within that territory (domestic production). *Gross National Product* includes the production owned by nationals (citizens) overseas. *Gross National Income* (GNI) is a variant of GNP. All three are frequently divided by total population to produce a rough measure of productivity per capita (person), and an even more approximate measure of average income.

Heavily Indebted Poor Countries (HIPC): Forty countries defined by the HIPC Initiative of the IMF and the World Bank as potentially eligible to receive debt relief on the basis that they have "a proven track record in implementing strategies focused on reducing poverty and building the foundation for sustainable economic growth."

Human Development Index: A combined measure of social development, based on life expectancy, literacy and enrolment in education, and GDP (PPP) per capita.

Industrialization: The process through which industrial capacity is created. The increased productivity, and increased range, of goods and services arising from industrialization bring the potential for higher living standards.

Industry: The mining, manufacturing and energy sectors of production. Also refers to a constant process of technical and social change that continually increases society's capacity to produce a wide range of goods.

Infectious disease: *see* **Communicable disease**

OECD: The Paris-based Organisation for Economic Co-operation and Development. Its 32 members, which represent the world's major free-market economies, meet for discussions, and make legally binding agreements.

Map projection: A representation of the globe on a flat surface. "Projections" involves compromise. This atlas uses the 1913 Winkel Tripel projection. The "Tripel" refers to the three elements of area, direction and distance. Cartographer Oswald Tripel minimized distortion in all three elements.

Non-communicable disease: A disease that cannot be caught from another person. The risk of developing certain of these diseases is known to be influenced by factors such as life-style.

Poverty: While conventional definitions focus on the absence of wealth or material possessions, research using the perspectives of poor people recognizes that poverty also involves vulnerability and exclusion from society.

Poverty gap: The depth of individual or household poverty, measured in terms of the distance between the poverty line and the income of an individual or household whose income is below the line.

Poverty line: A level of personal income below which someone is deemed to be living in poverty. These levels are often set nationally, either as a percentage of the average income or in relation to the price of basic goods. Internationally, the threshold of $1, or more recently, $1.25, a day is used.

Purchasing Power Parity: PPP rates of currency exchange take account of price differences between countries by comparing the cost of a common basket of commodities in every country. This facilitates comparisons of real values for income, poverty, and consumption.

Quartile: One of four equal parts (a quarter, or 25% of a whole).

Quintile: One of five equal parts (a fifth, or 20% of a whole).

Services: Intangible products such a banking, insurance, accounting, medicine, cleaning.

Years of life lost (YLL): Number of deaths multiplied by the remaining life expectancy at the age at which death occurs.

Sources

For sources available on the internet, in most cases only the root address has been given. To view the source, it is recommended that the reader types the title of the web page, database, or document into a search engine.

9–13 Introduction

Agarwal B, Humphries J, Robeyns I, editors. *Amartya Sen's work and ideas: A gender perspective.* Abingdon and New York: Routledge; 2005.

Davies J et al The global pattern of household wealth. *Journal of International Development* 1999;21:1-14.

Global reports: an overview of their evolution. ODS Staff Paper. New York: UNDP, Office of Development Studies; 2004.

HDI definitions and facts http://hdr.undp.org/en/statistics/indices/hdi/

McGillivray M, White H. Measuring development? The UNDP's Human Development Index. *Journal of International Development.* 2006;5(2):183-92.

Sen A. *Inequality re-examined.* Cambridge: Harvard University Press; 1992.

Sen A. *Development as freedom.* Oxford: Oxford University Press; 1999/2000.

Sen A. A decade of human development. In: First Global Forum on Human Development, New York; 1999 July. http://hdr.undp.org

State of the world's children 2009. UNICEF; 2009. www.unicef.org

Therborn, G, editor. *Inequalities of the world: new theoretical frameworks, multiple empirical approaches,* Introduction. London: Verso; 2006.

Therborn G. Killing fields of inequality: What are the contemporary causes of inequality in the world? *Soundings.* 2009;42:20-32. http://www.eurozine.com/articles/2009-10-02-therborn-en.html

Thomas A. Poverty and the end of development. In: Allen T, Thomas A, editors. *Poverty and development into the 21st century.* Oxford: Oxford University Press; 2000. pp.3-22.

HUMAN DEVELOPMENT INDEX COMPARISON OF INCOME AND HUMAN DEVELOPMENT
Human development report 2009. http://hdr.undp.org

RURAL–URBAN DIVIDE
China human development report 2005. www.undp.org.cn

Part 1 Economic Inequalities

Davies JB, Sandstrom S, Shorrocks A, Wolff EN. Estimating the level and distribution of global household wealth. UNU-WIDER Research Paper No. 2007/77. Latest version appears as, The world distribution of household wealth. *The Journal of International Development*; 2009.

Milanovic B. Global inequality recalculated. World Bank Policy Research Working Paper 5061. 2009 Sept.

16–17 Income
HISTORICAL RISE IN INCOME INEQUALITY
In 1820 the ratio...
Human development report 1999. http://hdr.undp.org

INCOME DISTRIBUTION *Human development report 2007/08.* Table 15. http://hdr.undp.org

INEQUALITY BETWEEN AND WITHIN COUNTRIES
The average income of the richest...
Income and pop data: World Bank's World Development Indicators www.wri.org (accessed 2009 Jan 13).

Decile data for developed countries: World Income Inequality Database www.wider.unu.edu

Decile data for developing countries: povCal Net database www.wri.org and other sources.

18–19 Household Wealth
Davies JB, Sandstrom S, Shorrocks A, Wolff EN. Estimating the level and distribution of global household wealth. UNU-WIDER Research Paper No. 2007/77. Latest version: The world distribution of household wealth. *The journal of international development*; 2009.

20–21 Consumption
Human development report 1998. http://hdr.undp.org

Food security in the United States: key statistics and graphics. www.ers.usda.gov (accessed June 2010).

Measure Demographic and Health Surveys. www.measuredhs.com

UNEQUAL CONSUMPTION
Shah A. Consumption and consumerism. *Global issues.* 2008 Sept 3 (accessed 2010 Feb 17). www.globalissues.org

EXPENDITURE ON FOOD
FAO. Food security statistics. Access to food. 2008 Oct 30 (accessed April 2010). www.fao.org

WHO CAN AFFORD HOUSEHOLD ASSETS
www.measuredhs.com

The richest fifth own 87%
HDR 1998. p.2.

22–23 Work & Unemployment
International Labor Organization. LABORSTA. http://laborsta.ilo.org

World development indicators; 2009 (accessed 2010 Apr 12). www.wri.org

Sutcliffe B. *100 ways of seeing an unequal world.* Zed Books; 2001.

Human development report 2007/8. Tables 20 and 21.

GENDER DIFFERENCES IN UNEMPLOYMENT
HDR Report 2007/8. Table 21. http://hdr.undp.org

HISTORICAL TREND
SECTORAL CONTRIBUTION TO WORLD'S GDP
GDP: World development indicators 2007.
Sector contribution: CIA World FactBook 2010. www.cia.gov

COMPARATIVE PRODUCTIVITY
World development indicators 2007.
In some countries, more than 70%...
In some countries, 60% are employed
HDR 2007/8.

24–25 Labour Migration
Human development report 2009. http://hdr.undp.org

Labor Migration. World Bank. Web. 8 Mar. 2010. http://web.worldbank.org

MIGRATION WITHIN CHINA
China human development report 2005. http://hdr.undp.org
http://chinadataonline.org

INTERNAL MIGRATION AND EMIGRATION
Human development report 2009, page 22.

DESTINATION OF INTERNATIONAL MIGRANTS
HDR 2009. p.30.

FINANCIAL BENEFITS OF MIGRATION
HDR 2009. p.50.

FINANCIAL CONSTRAINTS ON EMIGRATION
HDR 2009. p.25.

MONEY SENT HOME BY MIGRANTS
World Bank. Migration and development brief 11. http://econ.worldbank.org

Only 1 in 3...
HDR 2009. p.2.

International migrations: 214 million...
UN Economic and Social Affairs Population Division. International Migration Wallchart 2009. un.population.org
HDR 2009. p.2.

Part 2 Power Inequalities

Lukes S. *Power: a radical view*. London: Macmillan Press; 1974.

Human development report 2005. p.94. http://hdr.undp.org

Maddison A. *The world economy: a millennial perspective*. Paris: OECD; 2001

28–29 International Trade
EXPORT OF MANUFACTURED GOODS

World Trade Organization. International trade statistics 2009 (accessed 2010 Apr 29). www.wto.org

UNEQUAL TARIFFS

GTAP Version 6.0 database. www.gtap.org. Cited by Hertel TW, Keeney R. Chapter 2: What's at stake: the relative importance of import barriers, export subsidies and domestic support. The World Bank; 2006. http://siteresources.worldbank.org

Manufactured goods represent only 18%...

WRO. International Trade Statistics 2009. Table II.2.

COMMODITY DEPENDENCE

Page S, Hewitt A. *World commodity prices: still a problem for developing countries?* Overseas Development Institute; 2001.

UNCTAD. *Commodity yearbook 2003*. TD/B/CN.1/STAT/4. United Nations Conference on Trade and Development; 2003.

Both of the above cited by Agriculture and Natural Resources Team of DIFD; Gillson I, Wiggins S, Pandian N. Rethinking tropical agricultural commodities. UK Department for International Development (DIFD) and Overseas Development Institute; 2004. http://dfid-agriculture-consultation.nri.org

INSECURITY FOR COFFEE GROWERS

International Coffee Organization (ICO) www.ico.org

FAO Commodities and Trade Division. International commodity prices. www.fao.org (accessed 2010 May 8).

UNCTAD as cited by Common Fund for Commodities. 2005 Mar 21-23. Overview of the situation of commodities in developing countries. www.g77.org

Rich countries spend: $1 billion a day...

Human development report 2005. p.10. http://hdr.undp.org

30–31 Budget Priorities

Mackintosh M. Questioning the state. In: Wuyts M, Mackintosh M, Hewitt T, editors. *Development and public action*. Oxford University Press; 1992.

World Bank. *World development report 2006*. Oxford University Press; 2006. www.wri.org

BIG SPENDERS

The USA was responsible for 41%...

Stockholm International Peace Research Institute. *SIPRI yearbook 2009*. p.182. www.sipri.org

GOVERNMENT PRIORITIES

Education: UNESCO Institute for Statistics. http://stats.uis.unesco.org

Health: World development indicators online. www.wri.org

Military: The SIPRI Military Expenditure Database. http://milexdata.sipri.org

Countries with no armed forces: http://en.wikipedia.org (data checked for reliability)

SPENDING ON SOCIAL CARE

ILO Social Security Expenditure Database (2000-2007). www.ilo.org

Proportion of GDP spent on social security: Building decent societies. Rethinking the role of social security in state building. ILO; 2009. p.1. www.ilo.org

32–33 Government Action
MINIMUM WAGE

Minimum wage in Denmark...

List of minimum wages by country. Wikipedia (accessed 2010 Apr 28). http://en.wikipedia.org

2008 Country reports on human rights practices. US Department of State: Bureau of Democracy, Human Rights, and Labor (accessed 2010 Apr 28). www.state.gov

REDISTRIBUTION THROUGH TAXATION
DISTRIBUTION OF GOVERNMENT MONEY

Engel E, Galetovic A, Raddatz C. Taxes and income distribution in Chile: some unpleasant redistributive arithmetic. *Journal of development economics* 1999:59:155-92.

Goñi E, López JH, Servén L. Fiscal redistribution and income inequality: Latin America. The World Bank; 2008. www-wds.worldbank.org

Lindert K, Skoufias E, Shapiro J. Redistributing income to the poor and the rich: public transfers in Latin America and the Caribbean. The World Bank; 2005. http://siteresources.worldbank.org

LAND REFORM

Barraclough SL. Land reform in developing countries: the role of the state and other actors. United Nations Research Institute on Social Development; 1999. www.unrisd.org

Prosterman R, Mitchell R. Concept of land reform for Java. Paper presented at the seminar Rethinking Land Reform in Indonesia, 2002 May 8. On file with the Rural Development Institute. www.rdiland.org

34–35 Freedom & Democracy

Human development report 2002. http://hdr.undp.org

Djankov S, McLiesh C, Nenova T, Shleifer A. Who owns the media? Background paper prepared for World Development Report 2001/2002. www.worldbank.org

Corruptions perception index 2009 www.transparency.org

Governance matters 2009. Voice and accountability. http://info.worldbank.org

The economist intelligence unit index of democracy 2008. http://graphics.eiu.com

Kaufmann D, Kraay A, Mastruzzi M. Governance matters VIII: Aggregate and individual governance indicators: 1996-2008. The World Bank Development Research Group; 2009.

Peruzzotti E, Smulovitz C. Civil society, the media and internet as tools for creating accountability to poor and disadvantaged groups. Background paper for HDR 2002.

Bertrand JC. *A strategy for democracy*. Paris: Institut Francais de Presse; 2001.

Dreze J, Sen A. *Hunger and public action*. Oxford: Clarendon Press; 1989.

Sen A. *Development as Freedom*. Oxford: Oxford University Press; 1999.

Stanford encyclopedia of philosophy (SEP). Entries on Democracy and Corruption (accessed 2010 Apr 24). http://plato.stanford.edu

DEMOCRACY INDEX

Only 30% of the worlds...

The Economist intelligence unit index of democracy 2008.

Corruptions perceptions index 2009.

REGIONAL PRESS FREEDOM

Djankov S, McLiesh C, Nenova T, Shleifer A. Who owns the media? 2001. Background paper prepared for World Development Report 2001/2002.

Freedom House Press, 2009.

68% of Australia's newspaper market...

Jackson K. Media ownership regulation in Australia. Analysis and Policy Social Policy Group. 2006 May 30. www.aph.gov.au

36–37 Incarceration & Execution

Soaring costs for California's failing prison system. Quoting Governor Arnold Schwarzenegger. 2010 January 8. www.kpbs.org

Amnesty USA. Death penalty facts (accessed 2010 March). www.amnestyusa.org

Amnesty International. Abolitionist and retentionist countries. www.amnesty.org

The death penalty in 2008. www.amnesty.org

PUNISHMENT IN USA

www.clarkprosecutor.org (accessed 2010 March).

FBI. 2008 crime in the United States www.fbi.gov

CAPITAL PUNISHMENT

Death penalty: countries abolitionist for all crimes. www.amnesty.org

INCARCERATION

King's College, London, International Centre for Prison Studies. Prison brief. www.kcl.ac.uk

The USA has the largest...
40% of the world's prisoners...

Walmsley R. World prison population list. International Centre for Prison Studies. King's College London. www.kcl.ac.uk

Part 3 Social Inequalities

Vincent JA. *Inequality and old age.* London: UCL Press and NY: St Martin's Press; 1995

Sen G, Grown K. *Development crises and alternative visions: Third World women's perspectives.* London: Earthscan; 1988.

Whelan CT, Maitre B. Social class variation in risk: a comparative analysis of the dynamics of economic vulnerability. *British Journal of Sociology* 2008;59(4).

40–41 Gender

Blackden CM, Widon Q, editors. Gender, time, use, and poverty in Sub-Saharan Africa. World Bank Paper 73; 2006.

UNPAID DOMESTIC WORK
Women in India...

Elson D. Macroeconomic policy, employment, unemployment, and gender equality. In Ocampo JA, Jomo KS. editors. *Towards full and decent employment.* New York: United Nations; 2007. pp. 9-10.

MISSING DAUGHTERS

Seager J. *The atlas of the women in the world.* New York: Penguin; 2009. Original source: Census of India 2001.

WOMEN'S POLITICAL AND ECONOMIC PARTICIPATION AND POWER

Human development report 2009. Table K. pp.186-88. http://hdr.undp.org

Full information of GEM computation is in UNDP *HDR 2003.* p.345.

WOMEN EARNERS

Human development report 2007/8. Table 31. p.341. http://hdr.undp.org

In China in 2007, for every 100 boys...

China Statistical Yearbook 2007. Table 3-7. www.stats.gov.cn

42–43 Age

Shape of things to come. Population Action International; 2007. www.populationaction.org

Population handbook. Population Reference Bureau; 2004 (5th edition). www.prb.org

World population data sheet. Population Reference Bureau; 2009. www.prb.org

World population highlights. Population Reference Bureau; 2009. www.prb.org

Wolff P. Population and social conditions, EUROSTAT. Statistics in Focus. http://epp.eurostat.ecalso

Zaidi A. Poverty of elderly people in EU 25. European Centre Policy Brief; 2006. www.euro.centre.org.

AGE STRUCTURE TYPES

Shape of Things to Come, Population Action International; 2007.

COMPARATIVE AGE STRUCTURES
WOMEN LIVE LONGER
By 2050 90% of people...

UN Population Division. World population prospects. The 2008 revision. http://esa.un.org

ELDERLY WOMEN AT RISK OF POVERTY

At-risk-of-poverty rate after social transfers by age and gender. http://epp.eurostat.ec.europa.eu

44–45 Class

Bradley H. Changing social structures: class and gender. In: Hall S. *Modernity: an introduction to modern societies.* Oxford: Blackwell; 1996.

Portes A, Hoffman K. Latin American class structures: their composition and change during the neoliberal era. *Latin American Research Review 38;* 2003.

CLASS DIFFERENCES

Grussky DB, editor. *Social stratification: class, race and gender in sociological perspective.* Boulder: Westview; 1994. p.4, Table 1.

OWNER–EMPLOYEE RELATIONSHIP

Wright EO. *Class counts: comparative studies in class analysis.* Cambridge: Cambridge University Press; 1997. Fig. 2.1, p.47 and Table 2.4, p.62.

SOURCE OF INCOME

Dumenil G, Levy D. Neoliberal income trends. *New Left Review 30,* 2004 Nov-Dec. London.

Piketty T, Saez E. Income inequality in the United States, 1913-2002. In Atkinson AB, Piketty T, editors. *Top incomes of the 20th century.* Oxford: Oxford University Press; 2007. Table 1.

RURAL CLASS DISTRIBUTION

Bhattacharyya S. Class and the politics of participatory rural transformation in West Bengal: an alternative to World Bank orthodoxy. *Journal of Agrarian Change* 2007 June 3:348-81. p348-81, Table 1.

46–47 Race & Ethnicity

Human development report 2004. http://hdr.undp.org

State of the world's indigenous peoples 2009. www.un.org

Nepal human development report 2009. http://hdr.undp.org

Smith D. *The state of the world atlas.* London: Earthscan and New York: Penguin. 2004. p. 22-3.

International Fund for Agricultural Development, IFAD. www.ruralpovertyportal.org

Bureau of Justice Statistics: Prisoners in 2008. http://bjs.ojp.usdoj.gov

US Census Bureau. American Community Survey reports; 2004. www.census.gov

Prison Policy Initiative. www.prisonpolicy.org/graphs/raceinc.html

QUALITY OF LIFE

Cooke M. Indigenous well-being in four countries: An application of the UNDP'S Human Development Index to indigenous peoples in Australia, Canada, New Zealand, and the United States; 2007. www.biomedcentral.com

State of the world's indigenous peoples 2009. p.132

POVERTY RATES FOR ROMA IN EUROPE

UNDP. At risk: Roma and the displaced in Southeast Europe; 2006. p.18. http://europeandcis.undp.org

DISCRIMINATION AGAINST MINORITIES
Minorities suffering

Minorities at Risk Dataset: www.cidcm.umd.edu

EDUCATION IN MOTHER TONGUE
2,632 different languages...

HDR 2004, op. cit. p.34.

Indigenous peoples:...

IFAD. www.ruralpovertyportal.org

48–49 Child Labor

A future without child labour: global report under the follow-up to the ILO declaration on fundamental principles and rights at work International Labour Conference. 90th session; 2002. Report I (B). Geneva: International Labour Office. www2.ilo.org

Basu K, Tzaannatos Z. The global child labor problem: What do we know and what can we do? *The World Bank economic review* 2003;17(2):147-168.

Action against child labour 2008-2009: IPEC progress and future priorities. ILO; 2010 Feb.

The state of the world's children 2009. www.childinfo.org

Humphries J. Child labor: lessons from historical experience of today's industrialized countries. *World Bank economic review* 2003;17(2):175-196.

Satz D. Child labor: a normative perspective. *World Bank economic review* 2003;17(2):297-309.

WORKING CHILDREN

The end of child labor within reach. ILO report; 2006. www.ilo.org

DOMESTIC LABOR

Allais FB. Assessing the gender gap: Evidence from SIMPOC surveys. Geneva: ILO. 2009 July.

WORST FORMS OF CHILD LABOR

ILO 2002, op.cit.

CHILD LABOR

UNICEF global databases 2009: Table 9. www.childinfo.org

WORK VS SCHOOL

A future without child labour. op.cit. p.55.

Child laborers decreased by 11%...
12% of children aged 5–17 years...
65% of economically active children...

ILO 2006. op.cit.

Part 4 Inequalities of Access

Braun J, Vargas Hill R, Pandya-Lorch R,editors. The poorest and hungry: assessments, analyses, and actions. Washington DC: International Food Policy Research Institute; 2009.

World Bank's PovcalNet. http://research.worldbank.org

52–53 Poverty

Baulch B. The new poverty agenda: a disputed consensus (editorial). IDS Bulletin 37; 2006:82-90. http://community.eldis.org

CIESIN. Where the poor are: an atlas of poverty; 2006. http://sedac.ciesin.columbia.edu

Chambers R. Vulnerability, coping and policy (editorial introduction). IDS Bulletin 20; 2006:33-40. http://community.eldis.org

Collins D, Morduch J, Rutherford S, Ruthven O. *Portfolios of the poor: how the world's poor live on $2 a day.* Princeton University Press; 2009.

Global Distribution of Poverty: Poverty Mapping Project of the Center for International Earth Science Information Network. 2010. http://sedac.ciesin.columbia.edu

Narayan D, Pritchett L, Kapoor S. Moving out of poverty: success from the bottom up. The World Bank Poverty Reduction Group; 2005.

PovcalNet. 2010. http://web.worldbank.org

The World Bank. http://data.worldbank.org

POVERTY IN THE USA
www.census.gov/hhes/ www/poverty/microdata.htm

DESCENT INTO POVERTY
ESCAPE FROM POVERTY
Krishna A. For reducing poverty faster: target reasons before people. World Development 35:2007;1947-60.

DISTRIBUTION AND DEPTH OF POVERTY IN KENYA
Global Distribution of Poverty, op. cit. based on Poverty Gap Index [FGT(1)].

1 in 20...
National Center for Law and Economic Justice. www.nclej.org

Almost half...
World Bank Development Indicators 2008. www.globalissues.org

54–55 Hunger

World Food Programme: fighting hunger worldwide. World Food Programme. www.wfp.org

Crow B. Understanding famine and hunger. In: Allen T, Thomas A, editors. *Poverty and development into the 21st century,* Oxford: Oxford University Press; 2000.

Annual impact of under-nutrition...
Progress for children: a report card on nutrition. UNICEF; 2006.

PREVALENCE OF UNDERNOURISHMENT
FAO. Food security statistics 2010. www.fao.org

REGIONAL INCIDENCE OF CHRONIC HUNGER
FAO. *The state of food insecurity in the world 2008.* www.fao.org

RISE IN WORLDWIDE HUNGER
FAO *The state of food insecurity in the world 2009.* ftp://ftp.fao.org

CHILD MORTALITY AND MALNUTRITION

Dobie P, Yuksel N, Sanchez P, Swaminathan MS. Halving hunger: It can be done. UN Millennium Project; 2005. www.unmillenniumproject.org

More than 60%...
A child dies every...
FAO. *The state of food insecurity in the world 2006.* www.fao.org

More than 1 billion...
1.02 billion people hungry. FAO news release. 2009 June 19. www.fao.org

56–57 Household Water
PIPED CONNECTIONS
WHO/UNICEF. Joint monitoring programme. www.wssinfo.org

WATER COLLECTION
Data collected in 2006 for Nyando Springs study described in Crow B, Swallow B, Asamba I. *The springs of Nyando: water, social organization and livelihoods in Western Kenya.* Nairobi, Kenya: World Agroforestry Centre; 2009. www.worldagroforestry.org

URBAN–RURAL DIVIDE
WHO/UNICEF, op. cit.

PIPES FOR RICH PONDS FOR POOR
Data analyzed for selected countries from Measure Demographic and Health Surveys, USAID. www.measuredhs.com/

58–59 Energy
MILLIONS LACK ELECTRICITY
POOR RURAL ACCESS
More than 80%...
The energy access situation in developing countries. New York: UNDP and WHO; 2008. www.who.int

ENERGY CONSUMPTION
The World Bank. World development indicators (accessed 2010 May 3). www.worldbank.org

THE WORLD'S POOR PAY MORE
International Energy Agency. *World energy outlook 2002.* Paris: International Energy Agency; 2002. www.iea.org

The 18% of people...
International Energy Agency. *Key world energy statistics.* Paris: International Energy Agency; 2009. www.iea.org

60–61 Household Fuel

International Energy Agency. *Key world energy statistics.* Paris: International Energy Agency; 2009. www.iea.org

International Energy Agency. *World energy outlook 2004.* Paris: International Energy Agency; 2004. Chapter 10. www.iea.org

The World Bank. World development indicators (accessed 2010 May 3). www.worldbank.org

COMPARISON OF ENERGY CONSUMPTION AND SOURCES
HOUSEHOLD FUEL TRANSITION
International Energy Agency. *World energy outlook 2002.* Paris: International Energy Agency; 2002. www.iea.org

SOLID FUELS
NO ACCESS TO MODERN FUELS
3 billion people rely on...
Over 75% of people...
More than 70% of people...
The energy access situation in developing countries. New York: UNDP and WHO; 2008. www.who.int

62–63 Mobility

Roberts P, Shyam K, Rastogi C. *Rural access index: a key development indicator.* Washington DC: The International Bank for Reconstruction and Development; March 2006. http://siteresources.worldbank.org

The World Bank. Countries and regions data catalog (accessed 2010 April 2). http://data.worldbank.org/data-catalog

World Bank. Transport results measurements: global resources (accessed 2010 March 31). www.worldbank.org

RURAL ACCESS
1 billion rural people...
World Bank. Transport results measurement: rural access index (accessed 2010 March 6). www.worldbank.org

WOMEN BEAR THE BURDEN
Human development report 1998. http://hdr.undp.org

ROAD MOBILITY
People in high-income...
World Bank. World development indicators: traffic and congestion. www.worldbank.org

Population: http://data.worldbank.org www.dft.gov.uk

ROAD TRAFFIC DEATHS
WHO Global status report on road safety: time for action. Geneva: World Health Organization; 2009. www.who.int

64–65 Digital Divide

Human development report 2001. http://hdr.undp.org

International Telecommunication Union. *Measuring the information society;* 2009. www.itu.int

International Telecommunication Union. *Measuring the information society;* 2010, www.itu.int

2009 cell phone use...
Only 1 in 5 people...
ITU; 2010. op.cit.

RELATION BETWEEN ICT ACCESS AND COST
ITU; 2010. op.cit. p.10, 61, 54, 55, 57, 58.

WORLDWIDE ACCESS TO ICT
ITU; 2010. op.cit. p.19.

REGIONAL GROWTH OF INTERNET USE
1.8 billion people...
www.internetworldstats.com

Part 5 Health Inequalities

Causes of death: World Health Statistics 2010. www.who.int

Life expectancy www.gapminder.com

68–69 Life Expectancy

Kabir M. Determinants of life expectancy in developing countries. *The Journal of Developing Areas* 2008;41(2):185-204. http://muse.uq.ed.au/journals/journal_of_developing_areas

Kinsella KG. Changes in life expectancy 1900-1990. *American Journal of Clinical Nutrition* 1992; 55:1196S-1202S. www.ajcn.org

Piot P, Michael B, Peter DG, et al. The global impact of HIV/AIDS. *Nature* 2001 April; 419: 968-973. www.nature.com

Riley JC. Estimates of regional and global life expectancy, 1800-2001. *Population and Development Review* 2005;31(3):537-543. www.popcouncil.org

UC atlas of global inequality. Inequality and growth. 2003. http://ucatlas.ucsc.edu

WHO. Life expectancy at birth (years). WHO statistical information system; 2008 (accessed 2010 January 18). www.who.int

LIFE EXPECTANCY

WHO. World health statistics; 2009. WHO statistical information system (accessed 2010 February 16). www.who.int

RELATIONSHIP BETWEEN INCOME AND LIFE EXPECTANCY

Life expectancy data for 2000-2005: UN. Life expectancy at birth, both sexes combined (years); 2009 (accessed 2010 February 3). http://data.un.org

GDP per capita PPP$: World development indicators www.wri.org & CIA World Factbook (2008) www.cia.gov

70–71 Maternal Mortality

Khan, KS, Wojdyla D, Say L, et al. WHO analysis of causes of maternal death: a systematic review. *The Lancet* 2006; 367:1066-1074.

Rogo, KO, Oucho J, and Mwalali P. Maternal mortality. In: Jamison DT, Feachen RG, Makgoba MW, editors. *Disease and mortality in Sub-Saharan Africa*. 2nd ed. Washington DC: The World Bank; 2006.

The state of the world's children 2009. www.unicef.org

Maternal mortality in 2005: estimates developed by WHO, UNICEF, UNFPA and the World Bank; 2007. www.who.int

MATERNAL MORTALITY

A woman's chance...

Hill K, Thomas K, AbouZahr C, et al. (on behalf of the Maternal Mortality Working Group). Estimates of maternal mortality worldwide between 1990 and 2005: an assessment of available data. *The Lancet* 2007; 370:1311-19.

CAUSES OF MATERNAL DEATH

WHO. *The world health report 2005: make every mother and child count*. Geneva: World Health Organization; 2005. p. 62.

SKILLED ATTENDANCE LINKED TO INCOME

Gwatkin DR, Rutstein S, Johnson K, et al. Socio-economic differences in health, nutrition, and population within developing countries: an overview. *Journal of the American Medical Association* 2007 Oct 24/31;298(16). http://jama.ama-assn.org

SKILLED ATTENDANCE LINKED TO LOWER MATERNAL MORTALITY

Of the 534,000...

Hill K. et al. op.cit.

Gwatkin DR. et al. op.cit.

72–73 Child Mortality

Gwatkin DR, Rutstein S, Johnson K, et al. Socio-economic differences in health, nutrition, and population within developing countries: an overview. *Journal of the American Medical Association* 2007 Oct 24/31;298(16). http://jama.ama-assn.org

Gwatkin, DR, Wagstaff A, Yazbeck AS. *Reaching the poor with health, nutrition, and population services: what works, what doesn't, and why*. Washington DC: The World Bank; 2005.

Leon DA, Walt G. *Poverty, inequality, and health: an international perspective*. Oxford: Oxford University Press; 2001.

Fotso J, Ezeh AC, Madise NJ, et al. Infant mortality, access to safe water and full vaccination in Kenya. *BMC Public Health* 2007;7:218 www.biomedcentral.com

The state of the world's children 2009. Table 10. www.unicef.org

Countdown to 2015. *Tracking progress in maternal, newborn, and child survival: the 2008 report*. www.countdown2015mnch.org

UNEQUAL CHANCE OF SURVIVAL

WHO statistical information system. www.who.int/whosis

35% of deaths...

Black RE, et al. for the Maternal and Child Undernutrition Study Group. Maternal and child undernutrition: Global and regional exposures and health consequences. *The Lancet* 2008 January 17; p.5-22.

CHILD DEATHS

The state of the world's children 2009. Table 1. www.unicef.org

TRENDS IN CHILD MORTALITY

1 in 7 children...

You D, Wardlaw T, Salama P, et al. Levels and trends in under-5 mortality, 1990-2008.

The Lancet 2010 Jan 9; 375(9709):100-103.

Around 17 children...

UNICEF Millennium Development Goal 4: Reduce child mortality. www.unicef.org

CAUSES OF DEATH

Bryce J, et al. and the WHO Child Health Epidemiology Reference Group. WHO estimates of the causes of death in children. *The Lancet* 2005;365:1147-52.

74–75 Access to Healthcare

Krishna, A. For reducing poverty faster: target reasons before people. *World Development* 2007; 35(11):1947-1960.

UNEQUAL BENEFIT

Filmer D. *The incidence of public expenditures on health and education*. Washington DC: The World Bank; 2003 (background note for *World development report 2004 – Making services work for poor people*). http://www-wds.worldbank.org

PRIVATE HEALTHCARE

INEQUALITY OF PROVISION

WHO. World health statistics 2009. www.who.int/whosis

RURAL–URBAN DIVIDE

WHO. *Global atlas of the health workforce*; 2009. http://apps.who.int/globalatlas

UNEQUAL ACCESS

Gwatkin DR, Rutstein S, Johnson K, et al. Socio-economic differences in health, nutrition, and population within developing countries: an overview. *Journal of the American Medical Association* 2007 Oct 24/31;298 (16). http://jama.ama-assn.org

76–77 Infectious Diseases

WHO. *The top 10 causes of death*; 2004. www.who.int

Eberstadt, N. The Future of AIDS. *Foreign Affairs* 2002 Nov-Dec:81.6: 22.

Collins, J and Rau B. *AIDS in the context of development*. Geneva: United Nations Research Institute for Social Development; 2000.

WHO. *World health statistics 2009*. Part I: Health-related millennium development goals. www.who.int/whosis

AVERT. *Averting HIV and AIDS*. AVERT; 2010. www.avert.org/

WHO. *2009 Update tuberculosis facts*. http://who.org

UNFPA. *State of world population*; 2002. www.unfpa.org

Gwatkin DR, Rutstein S, Johnson K, et al. Socio-economic differences in health, nutrition, and population within developing countries: an overview. *Journal of the American Medical Association* 2007 Oct 24/31; 298 (16). http://jama.ama-assn.org

WHO. *Gender inequalities and HIV*; 2008. www.who.int

PREVALENCE OF DISEASE

WHO. *World malaria report; 2008*. http://who.int

HIV/AIDS survey indicators database (accessed 2010 April). www.measuredhs.com

UNAIDS and WHO. *2008 Report on the global AIDS epidemic*, Annex 1. Joint United Nations Programme on HIV/AIDS. http://data.unaids.org

WHO. *Global tuberculosis control 2009*. www.who.int

GENDER IMBALANCE
HIV/AIDS survey indicators database. op.cit.

HIV/AIDS has reduced...
UNFPA. Population and development strategy series, number 8. www.unfpa.org

In Sub-Saharan Africa...
UNAIDS and WHO. *2008 Report on the global AIDS epidemic*. op.cit.

ECONOMIC IMPACT
Sachs J, Malaney P. The economic and social burden of malaria. *Nature* 2002 February 7:680-685.

Treatment of malaria...
WHO. *Fact sheet number 94: Malaria*. www.who.int

9.2 million people...
WHO. *Global tuberculosis control: surveillance, planning, financing*; 2008. www.who.int

Part 6 Educational Inequalities

EFA Global Monitoring Reports; 2006, 2007, 2008, 2009, 2010. www.unesco.org

80–81 Literacy
EFA Global Monitoring Report – *Literacy for life*. UNESCO; 2006. www.unesco.org

Lloyd CB, Hewett P. *Educational inequalities in the midst of widespread poverty: diversity across Africa in primary school completion*. Population Council; 2009. www.popcouncil.org

GENDER DISPARITY
UNESCO Institute for Statistics. http://stats.uis.unesco.org

LITERACY
16% of people...
Human development report 2009. http://hdr.undp.org

QUALITY OF EDUCATION
INCOME AND EDUCATIONAL ATTAINMENT
Lloyd CB, Hewett P. op.cit.

82–83 Barriers to Education
MARGINALIZATION OF ETHNIC GROUPS
UNESCO. *EFA global monitoring report 2009*. www.unesco.org

ENROLLMENT IN PRIMARY EDUCATION
LACK OF OPPORTUNITIES
FAMILY CIRCUMSTANCES
18% of children...
UNESCO. *EFA global monitoring report*

2010. www.unesco.org

DISABILITY PREVENTS ACCESS TO EDUCATION
Kobainé, J. *La non-scolarisation des enfants issus de populations marginalisées au burkina faso: ampleur, causes et initiatives des pouvoir publics*. UNESCO; 2009. http://undesdoc.unesco.org

84–85 Early Childhood Care & Education
Heckman JJ. Perspective: skill formation and the economics of investing in disadvantaged children. *Science* 2006 June 30; 312(5782):1900-1902.

UNESCO. World Conference on Early Childhood Care & Education; 2010. www.unesco.org

Association for Childhood Education International. http://acei.org/

MOTHER'S EDUCATION COUNTS
THE POOR MISS OUT
Nonoyama-Tarumi Y, Loaiza E, Engle P. Inequalities in attendance in organized early learning programmes in developing societies: findings from household surveys. *British Association for International and Comparative Education* 2009 May; 39(3):385-409.

PRE-PRIMARY EDUCATION
UNESCO. *EFA global monitoring report 2010*. www.unesco.org

BENEFITS OF INVESTMENT IN EARLY CHILDHOOD
Heckman J, Grunewald R, Reynolds A. The dollars and cents of investing early: cost-benefit analysis in early care and education. *Zero to Three* 2006 July. http://main.zerotothree.org

Children in urban Burundi...
UNESCO. *EFA global monitoring report 2007*. p.111. www.unesco.org

Part 7 Environmental Inequalities

Environmental Performance Index (EPI). http://epi.yale.edu

88–89 Climate Change
CUMULATIVE CO₂ EMISSIONS
World Resources Institute. Climate analysis indicators tool. http://cait.wri.org

CO₂ EMISSIONS
US Energy Information Administration. US emissions data. www.eia.doe.gov/environment.html

STORMS, FLOODS AND DROUGHTS
POOREST LOSE MOST
Human development report 2007/2008. p.75. http://hdr.undp.org

Developing countries are...
HDR Report 2007/2008. op.cit. p. 8.

90–91 Deforestation
Barreto P. *Human pressure on the Brazilian*

Amazon forests. World Resources Institute; 2006.

The state of the forest: Indonesia. Bogor, Indonesia: Forest Watch Indonesia, and Washington DC: Global Forest Watch; 2002.

Fearnside PM. Deforestation in Amazonia. *The encyclopedia of earth*; 2007. www.eoearth.org

FAO. *Global forest resources assessment 2010*. www.fao.org

Geist HJ, Lambin EF, What drives tropical deforestation? LUCC Report Series Number 4; 2001.

Lambin EF, Geist HJ. Regional differences in tropical deforestation. *Environment* 2006 July/Aug; 45(6).

World Bank. *Forests sourcebook*, 2008.

Project Catalyst. Towards the inclusion of forest-based mitigation in a global climate agreement. www.project-catalyst.info

Seneca Creek Associates. Illegal logging and global wood markets: the competitive impact on the US wood products industry; 2004 Nov. www.illegal-logging.info

FAO. *The major significance of minor forest products*; 1990. www.fao.org.

FAO. *Global forestry resources management*. www.fao.org

MAIN CAUSES OF DEFORESTATION
Lambin EF, Geist HJ. op.cit. p.23.

DEFORESTATION AND REFORESTATION
www.fao.org

ILLEGAL LOGGING
Seneca Creek Associates. op.cit. Table 5.

60 million indigenous people...
World Bank, *Forests sourcebook*. op.cit. p.15.

Brazil and Indonesia accounted for 68%...
www.fao.org

92–93 Air Pollution & Health
WHO. Indoor air pollution: Pollution and exposure level; 2010 (accessed 2010 March 17). www.who.int

WHO. Indoor air pollution: Health effects; 2010 (accessed 2010 March 17). www.who.int

WHO. Media Centre: Indoor air pollution and health; 2010 (accessed 2010 March 02). www.who.int

Tobacco Atlas. Secondhand smoking. www.tobaccoatlas.org

DISEASE AND DEATH
WHO. *Deaths and DALYs attributable to three environmental risk factors*; 2002 (accessed 2010 Feb 25). www.who.int/

AIR POLLUTION IN THE HOME
Joint UNDP and ESMAP Program. *India: access of the poor to clean household fuels*; July 2003.

800,000 children younger than five...
WHO. *The world health report 2002*. p.69. www.who.int

MOST POLLUTED CITIES
World Bank. World development indicators: Air pollution; 2007 (accessed 2010 15 March). http://econ.worldbank.org
DEATHS FROM OUTDOOR POLLUTION
WHO. Regional burden of disease due to indoor air pollution; 2002. www.who.int
Urban air pollution caused 800,000 deaths
WHO. *The world health report 2002.* op.cit. p.69.

94–95 Water & Health
Fewtrell L, et al. Water, sanitation, and hygiene interventions to reduce diarrhoea in less developed countries: a systematic review and meta-analysis. *Lancet Infectious Diseases* 2005; 5(1): 42-52.
Prüss-Üstün A, Bos R, Gore F, et al. *Safer water, better health.* WHO; 2008. www.who.int
WHO. *Deaths and DALYs attributable to water, sanitation & hygiene*; 2002. www.who.int
WHO and UN Children's Fund Joint Monitoring Programme for Water Supply and Sanitation. *Progress on drinking water and sanitation: special focus on sanitation.* New York: UNICEF & Geneva:WHO; 2008.
UN. *The millennium development goals report*; 2008. www.un.org/millenniumgoals
DIARRHEAL DISEASE BURDEN
WHO. 2002 op.cit.
POPULATION WITHOUT IMPROVED SANITATION
Joint Monitoring Programme 2008 op.cit.
DISEASES CAUSED BY POOR WATER, SANITATION AND HYGIENE
Prüss-Üstün A. et al. op.cit.
IMPACT OF INTERVENTIONS
Prüss-Üstün A. et al. op.cit.
Fewtrell L. et al. op.cit.
MDG PROGRESS
Joint Monitoring Program. *Progress on sanitation and water;* 2010 update. WHO & UNICEF: 2010. http://unwater.org

Part 8 Moving Towards Equality
Bowles S, Gintis H. The inheritance of inequality. In: Bowles S, Gintis H, Osborne Groves M. editors. *Unequal chances.* New York: Russell Sage Foundation; 2005.
Dreze J. Sen A. Hunger and public action. Oxford: Clarendon Press; 1989.
Pew Foundation. Economic Mobility Project. An initiative of the Pew Charitable Trust. www.economicmobility.org
Hertz T. Rags, riches, and race: the intergenerational economic mobility of black and white families in the United States. In: Bowles S et al. op. cit.

Hertz T. *Understanding mobility in America.* Center for American Progress Report; June 2006.
Jenkins R. Political economy of industrialisation: a comparison of Latin American and East Asian newly industrialising countries. *Development and Change* 1991:22;197-231.
Milanovic B. Global inequality of opportunity: How much of our income is determined at birth?. Development Research Group Report. World Bank; 2008 June.
Therborn G. Killing fields of inequality: What are the contemporary causes of inequality in the world? *Soundings* 2009:42;20-32.
UN. *The millennium development goals report;* 2010. www.un.org/millenniumgoals

Part 9 Data, Definitions & Sources

Demographic and Health Surveys: www.measuredhs.com
Sen A. *Development as freedom.* Oxford University Press; 1999/2000.
UNICEF Multiple Indicator Cluster Surveys www.unicef.org
Progress for children. UNICEF; 2009 Sept.

Table 1: Income, Expenditure & Earnings
Population and GNI: World Bank Indicators http://data.worldbank.org [downloaded 2010 July 26]
Gini index: *Human development report* 2007-08. Table 15. http://hdr.undp.org
Wealth: Davies JB, Sandstrom S, Shorrocks A, Wolff EN. Estimating the level and distribution of global household wealth. UNU-WIDER Research Paper No. 2007/77. Latest version: The world distribution of household wealth. *The journal of international development;* 2009.
Human Development Index: *Human development report 2009.* http://hdr.undp.org
Food expenditure: FAO. Food security statistics. Access to food. 2008 Oct 30 (accessed April 2010). www.fao.org
Military expenditure: Education: UNESCO Institute for Statistics http://stats.uis.unesco.org; Health: World development indicators online www.wri.org; Military: The SIPRI Military Expenditure Database http://milexdata.sipri.org
National minimum wage: List of minimum wages by country.Wikipedia (accessed 2010 Apr 28). http://en.wikipedia.org
2008 Country reports on human rights practices. US Department of State: Bureau of Democracy, Human Rights, and Labor. (accessed 2010 Apr 28) www.state.gov

Healthcare: World Health Statistics. World Health Organization; 2009. www.who.int
Child labor: UNICEF global databases 2009: Table 9. www.childinfo.org

Table 2: Access to Health & Services
Life expectancy: World health statistics. World Health Organization; 2009. Downloaded 2010 February 16. www.who.int/whosis/whostat/2009/en
Maternal mortality: Hill K et al. Estimates of maternal mortality worldwide between 1990 and 2005: an assessment of available data. *Lancet* 2007;370:1311-19.
Child mortality: *State of the world's children 2009.* Table 1 Basic indicators. www.unicef.org [Downloaded 2010 March 29]
Undernourished: Food security statistics. 2010. www.fao.org
Piped water supply: WHO/UNICEF. Joint monitoring programme. www.wssinfo.org
Diarrheal disease: World Health Organization. Deaths and DALYs attributable to water, sanitation & hygiene (2002). www.who.int [Downloaded 2010 Feb 25]
Energy consumption: The World Bank. World development indicators [Downloaded 2010 May 3] www.worldbank.org
CO_2 emissions: www.eia.doe.gov/environment.html
Modern fuels: United Nations Development Programme and the World Health Organization. *The energy access situation in developing countries.* New York: UNDP and WHO; 2008. www.who.int
Mobility: Rural Access Index. [Downloaded 2010 Mar 6] www.worldbank.org
Literacy: *Human development report 2009.* http://hdr.undp.org.
Primary enrollment: EFA Global monitoring report 2010. Reaching the marginalized. Paris:UNESCO; 2010. http://unesdoc.unesco.org

Index